Life Expectancy Issues Across the Globe

Factors That Affect Human Life Span

By

Louis N. Chude

Table of Contents

Introduction

Welcome to life expectancy. This is a book about how and why people age and die. It's referred to as "womb to tomb."

However, it is the rationale of individuals' longevity and populations' life expectancy which are the basis for individuals' and populations' longevity and the amount of healthy and productive life years. Life expectancy is the most popular criterion for comparing the survival experience of populations. It's an estimate of the number of years a person has left to live, and it's a crucial factor for making clinical decisions in primary care.

Consider your life 5, 10, or even 15 years ago. How have you changed or evolved through time? What aspects of yourself have remained the same? You have likely changed physically; you may have gotten taller and gained weight. However, you may have also experienced changes in your way of thinking and problem-solving. For instance, comparing how 6-year-olds, 16-year-old, and 46-year-olds think and reason reveals significant cognitive change. Their perspectives on others and the world likely differ significantly. Consider friendship as an illustration.

The 6-year-old may believe that a friend is someone with whom one can have fun and play. A 16-year-old may seek out acquaintances who can assist them in gaining status or notoriety. And while the 46-year-old may have acquaintances, they rely on family members for activities and confiding. You may have also undergone a psychosocial transformation. The world's average life expectancy has continuously increased over the past few decades. Before the twentieth century, contagious infections were a common cause of death. This book will provide further details.

This book examines the following metric trends:

The average number of years an individual is projected to live is based on the current mortality rate population (births plus deaths)

Healthy anticipated life span (Depending on current mortality rates and the prevalence of good or healthy health, the average number of years that a person can anticipate to live in a condition of self-assessed health)

The average number of unhealthy years lived (the difference between average life span and healthy life expectancy)

The percentage of years spent in poor health (years spent in poor health as a proportion of life expectancy) Natural growth = Birth-Death)

On average, two populations may spend 15 years in bad health, which may be a quarter of life for a group with a longevity of 60 but only one-sixth of life for a population with a 90-year life expectancy. In the current life tables, the highest average life expectancy at birth is 81.9 years for men in Switzerland and 87.3 years for women in Japan. The lowest average life expectancy at birth is 63.9 years in South Africa (OECD 2020). Life expectancies worldwide are very heterogeneous. Regardless of the lengths of lives, a crucial question is how healthy life years will be when life expectancy keeps increasing.

However, increases in life expectancy have long been considered the most powerful evidence of improvements in health. Despite its popularity, life expectancy has the important shortcoming that it is only a measure of mortality (ignoring the health status of those who remain alive), and it needs to provide insights into whether improving health equally matches the rate of decreasing mortality. Since 1950, life expectancy has only grown in just 60 years, and individuals mediate from the date indicated to 2010.

In the world population, average life expectancy increased by 20 years, allowing an average of 66 years for each inhabitant of the planet. This trend, far from dwindling, will only increase in the next few years, anticipating that, in 2050, the world average will rise by ten years.

However, some studies believe that life expectancy in Africa is relatively high in comparison. As a result of its low level of industrialization, Africa has natural environments that are less polluted than those on other continents. It also has geographical and, by extension, overall weather advantages over different continents.

Conversely, some also argued that life expectancy in Africa is relatively low viz-à-viz other continents due to a high level of environmental hazards, such as carbon dioxide (CO_2) emissions, inadequate attention to hygiene, insufficient nutritional knowledge, and poor nutrition health care facilities, low-income status, etc. Mobile phones' battery percentage doesn't just decrease without reason. This book will highlight some reasons that reduce or increase life expectancy.

Before we proceed into the full details, glimpse what I'm about to unfold in the book.

Over the years, there have been controversies on who determines the longevity of children– mother or father, or if it is inherited from either. Disagreements about lifespan are caused by genetics. Or if the parental lifespan is linked to children's chances of reaching high age. This book will answer all our philosophical questions.

Longevity genes are an emerging field of inquiry. Approximately 25% of the diversity in the human lifespan is attributed to genetics. However, which genes and how they contribute to longevity still need to be fully understood. Some of the frequent variants (called polymorphisms) associated with long life lengths are present in the Apolipoprotein E (APOE) and Common effluent treatment plants (CETP) genes, although not in all individuals with remarkable longevity. It is probable that polymorphisms in numerous genes, some unexplained, work in concert to contribute to a long life. Longer life expectancies tend to run in families, indicating that genetics, lifestyle, or both are significant in determining longevity.

Scientists hypothesize that lifestyle influences health and longevity more than heredity for the first seven or eight decades. Some individuals can obtain a healthy old age by eating well, not drinking too much alcohol, avoiding cigarettes, and staying physically active. However, heredity is increasingly essential in maintaining health as individuals reach their eighties and beyond.

Additionally, the likelihood of reaching a ripe old age is transmitted from parents to offspring in a modest but substantial manner. Individual resilience inheritance parallels the inheritance of longevity. As a result of adversity and formative experience, we hypothesize that an individual's resilience emerges early in life. This results in a trajectory distinct from social class trajectories that span generations. A theory of longevity inheritance should incorporate new findings from epigenetics and social epidemiology with existing ideas of general vulnerability, frailty, and resistance. Because education, occupation, and income predict health and survival, we should also expect such characteristics in the parental generation to predict the next generation's health prospects, resulting in an "inheritance of longevity." However, this influence from previous generations may be considerably broader than that of working through the children's education, occupation, and income. Variation in mortality risk within social groups is great. To understand the "inheritance of longevity," we need a conceptual framework that identifies those within-class influences.

Men's life expectancy at birth was positively affected by the hospital admission ratio and national health insurance costs and negatively by the rate of the requirement of care certification and alcohol consumption. Men's life expectancy at age 65 was positively affected by the income-to-medical expenses ratio and hospitalization treatment ratio and negatively by requiring care certification rate, smoking rate, and obesity rate. Women's life expectancy at birth was positively affected by population coverage and hospitalization treatment ratio and negatively by women's heart disease mortality rate, requiring care certification rate, and smoking rate. Women's life expectancy at age 65 was positively affected by late-stage elderly medical costs and the number of doctors, and negatively by requiring care certification rate and air pollution. Principal component 1 indicated an "aging high-medical-resource society," main component 2 indicated "high mortality from heart disease," and principal component 3 indicated the "degree of risk factor."

Nevertheless, we observe a steady lifespan extension in modern societies, especially among women, partly based on falling mortality rates across their long post-reproductive period. That children tend to live longer than their parents are likely to be determined both by what experience parents bring to the next generation and by the improved life circumstances of the children themselves in their childhood and adult life.

Longevity is heritable. However, this primarily pertains to individuals from families with numerous members in the top 10 percent of their birth cohort's survival. The key to longevity can be discovered in these families' genes.

From 1960 to 2010, a review of birth and death statistics for adults over 65 showed that every 25 years, the average age of death for individuals who survive to be older than 65 greatly increased by three years. This implies that, on average, people may expect to live approximately six years longer than their grandparents.

In addition, this tendency remained relatively consistent across the 50 years and in each of the 20 counties. Minor fluctuations in the rate at which lifespans rose were induced by factors such as medical advancements, but these differences eventually balanced out over time. The growth in lifespan during any given decade was comparable.

Before we move forward with the chapters of this book, let's highlight some factors affecting life expectancy in some countries. Let's start with the United States. Why is the average lifespan lower in the United States than people in other wealthy countries, despite paying so much more for health care?

Despite paying far more for healthcare, Americans have a lower life expectancy than citizens of other wealthy nations. We investigate a variety of reasons that may explain this disparity.

In the 1970s, the United States did not stand out, but now it does since its life expectancy has increased considerably more slowly than other nations. Simultaneously, health expenditures in the United States climbed far faster, especially after the mid-1980s. As a result of these two rare occurrences, the United States followed the chart's significantly flattered course.

The United States of America invests more money in health care than any other country, yet its population has a shorter life expectancy than wealthy nations that spend much less. Smoking, obesity, killings, opioid overdoses, suicides, traffic accidents, and infant mortality rates are greater among Americans. In addition, Americans with lesser earnings die younger than poor individuals in other wealthy nations due to greater poverty and a lack of access to healthcare.

In the United States, smoking is one-factor determining life expectancy. Tobacco smoking is currently one of the world's major health issues. Every year, 8.1 million individuals die prematurely due to smoking. Half of them are younger than 70 years old. Between 1950 and 2000, smoking was pervasive in today's wealthy nations. In the United States, smoking was more prevalent than in Europe or Japan. Americans died at a higher rate due to the effects of tobacco (most of these died from lung cancer).

A further factor is obesity. Moreover, two-thirds of Americans are overweight (70%), and more than one-third are obese (36%). Obesity is a major risk component for several leading causes of mortality in wealthy nations, including cardiovascular disease, diabetes, some malignancies, and stroke. The US death rate from obesity-related conditions is estimated to be three times that of other countries. It will be essential for all nations to achieve headway against obesity to improve the health of the United States population; this is particularly crucial.

The United States has a far higher homicide rate than other wealthy nations.

As most homicide victims are young, this contributes to the United States' lower life expectancy than other prosperous nations. This is significant but cannot explain the growing disparity in life expectancy between the United States and other nations over time. In recent decades, homicide rates in the United States have decreased more than in other wealthy countries. The more significant reduction in homicide rates in the United States has lessened the relative disparity in life expectancy between nations.

Moreover, suicide is one factor that influences life expectancy in the World. Suicide rates have climbed marginally over the past decade. This is not the situation in many other wealthy nations; you can move to any country. Additionally, global suicide rates have declined significantly in recent years. The United States stands out, especially concerning suicides caused by firearms, which are significantly less common in countries worldwide. It's now an annual US festival, especially for cans. Most of them died of suicide.

Suicides are also a few causes of mortality, with a high risk for younger individuals. The age breakdown of suicides and the fact that suicide rates are growing in the United States while declining in many other wealthy nations explain why this is another reason why people die that adds to the disparity in life expectancy I am attempting to describe.

All continents and countries have different and similar factors which reduce life expectancies.

People in Sub-Saharan Africa, for example, are far less well-off and more likely to die early than those in affluent regions of the world. On the contrary, it is crucial to recognize that individuals who live past the age of 5 have a strong probability of surviving to approximately 60. Saving a life from even a single cause of death means protecting a person who is likely to live for a considerable amount of time longer.

Due to widespread poverty, starvation, and disease, most African nations continue to have the lowest life expectancy in the world.

The HIV/AIDS epidemic has become one of Africa's most significant health problems. HIV/AIDS has tragically claimed countless lives in Africa, a substantial factor in the continent's poor life expectancy. At the height of the crisis, it was challenging to treat these diseases. Therefore, many Africans sadly perished. Because HIV/AIDS has been such a significant problem, much research has been conducted to combat it. Medication and therapy advancements have helped Africans and others worldwide tackle the AIDS pandemic. Not only is there now medication to help suppress the condition, but it has also become far cheaper for everyone, especially those in developing nations.

Despite being an epidemic, HIV/AIDS was not the only difficulty African nations faced. Malaria was another factor affecting life expectancy in Africa. However, efforts have been made to address this issue as well. Since 2000, the World Health Organization (WHO) in Africa has recorded a 66% decline in malaria prevalence. Malaria incidence among African children under five has fallen by 71%. This is significant because more African youngsters are surviving. Prior to these advancements, HIV/AIDS and malaria took the lives of numerous children younger than five.

In parts of sub-Sahara Africa, cultism can also be counted as one factor affecting lifespan. 65% of the youths leaving this world untimely are cultists. They kill themselves before reaching 50 years old.

Additionally, environmental pollution can impact human longevity. In a variety of ways, environmental deterioration can negatively affect population health. Severe outdoor air pollution is responsible for increased chronic diseases (such as heart disease, asthma, and lung cancer) and early deaths. Others have determined that environmental deterioration increases the likelihood of waterborne infections such as dengue fever and malaria. Environmental pollution increases the ecosystem's unpredictability, which raises the possibility of floods and droughts. As a result, environmental degradation may result in unfavorable fluctuations in food production and water quality, increasing mortality, especially among newborn and elderly populations and vulnerable individuals from lower socio-economic backgrounds. It may not be surprising that people's diets have a significant impact. One thing is to have a general idea of what to eat for health, but the amount of information available can be overwhelming.

However, it may be crucial to avoid a low-protein diet to maintain a healthy weight and prevent weakness at older ages. Compared to individuals who received a low-protein diet, those who consumed animal-based, high-protein nutrition were more likely to die from cancer and 74% more likely to die from any disease.

Good nutrition is vital for maintaining the health of present and future generations throughout their lifespans. A balanced diet promotes optimal growth and development in children and minimizes their risk of chronic disorders. Adults who consume a nutritious diet have a lower risk of obesity, heart disease, or developing type 2 diabetes and some malignancies and live longer. A healthy diet can aid individuals with chronic diseases in managing their conditions and preventing complications.

In the absence of healthy options, however, individuals may end up settling for meals that are higher in calories and have fewer nutrients. Low-income areas and certain racial and ethnic groups frequently lack access to convenient, inexpensive, nutritious food sources.

Most Americans lack a nutritious diet and consume too much sodium, saturated fat, and sugar, making them more likely to get chronic diseases. Less than 1 in 10 adolescents and adults, for example, consume enough amounts of fruits and vegetables. In addition, 6 out of 10 children ages 2 to 19 and 5 out of 10 adults eat at least one sugary drink daily.

You are already drooling. This is hardly a particle of sand compared to what we have decoded in this book.

Sit in a conducive room with a glass of coffee and enjoy the book.

Chapter 1

Life Expectancy

Everything that has breathed must surely face death. In life, human beings are not created to be immortal.

According to the Association of American Psychologists (AAP), individuals are not concerned about living a long time but know that they can live calmly and happily on earth. It is observable that they have never paid so much attention to tactics for living the maximum number of years conceivable for humans.

Life expectancy is the most popular criterion for comparing the survival experience of populations. It estimates the remaining years of a person's life and is crucial in primary care clinical decision-making.

Life expectancy is influenced by an individual's particular health history, genetics, and lifestyle, whereas lifespan is constant for all living individuals. Life expectancy is influenced by an individual's health history, genetics, and lifestyle, whereas lifespan is constant for all living individuals.

According to DR. Ananya Mandal, MD, she said "Life expectancy refers to the statistically average number of years an individual is predicted to live. This statistical average is based on the entire population, including those who die soon before labor, shortly after childbirth, during adolescence or adulthood, die in combat, and survive to a ripe old age."

There is a disagreement that life expectancies should be estimated after childhood when it is possible to have a better grasp on a lifetime. For instance, the "Roman Lifestyle Expectancy" table illustrates how life expectancy differs dramatically after childhood.

At birth, life expectancy was twenty-one years, but by the time a kid reached the age of five, it had increased to forty-two years.

Other studies, such as "Dead at Forty" and "Plymouth Plantation," have also demonstrated the expected increase in life expectancy between childhood and adulthood.

Whether calculating the life expectancy of plants, animals, or humans, tables known as actuarial tables or mortality tables are utilized. Using people as an example, I forecast the probability that an individual of a certain age would pass away before their next birthday. Several points can be determined from this data, including:

The probability of individuals living to a particular age given

The estimated years of existence are expected to be lived by individuals of varying ages.

Jeanne Calment of France achieved the oldest known human life span of one hundred and twenty years. This is the maximum lifespan, the longest period that any human has ever lived.

Many people in late adulthood have higher health and social well-being than the typical person and would be aging optimally. Others, on the other hand, suffer from bad health and dependency to a higher level than typical. When examining large populations, the WHO (2016) calculates how many comparable years of full health a newborn baby is projected to experience on average. This age is referred to as the Healthy Life Expectancy since it considers the current age-specific mortality, morbidity, and disability risks. Global Healthy Life Expectancy was 63.1 years in 2015, up from 58.5 years in 2000. At 52.3 years, WHO's Western Pacific Region had the highest healthy life expectancy at 68.7 years, while WHO's African Region had the lowest.

Some of the oldest-old are centenarians, or people 100 and older; others are supercentenarians, or those 110 and older. Globally, there were about 500,000 centenarians in 2015, and it is projected that this age group will increase to nearly 3.7 million by 2050. The most significant number of living centenarians are found in the United States, but Japan and Italy have the most per capita. Most centenarians enjoyed better health than their contemporaries as they aged, and the beginning of any severe sickness or impairment was frequently delayed until their 90s. In addition, 25% of centenarians were free of major chronic conditions such as depression, osteoporosis, cardiovascular disease, respiratory sickness, or dementia. Centenarians are more likely to undergo a swift terminal decline in old age, indicating that for most of their adulthood and even their senior adult years, they are relatively healthy compared to most other elderly individuals.

If mortality increases in a population, Life expectancy declines. Conversely, if mortality declines, Life expectancy increases, the measure is age-standardized and thus commonly employed for international comparisons of population health. In this book, I investigate Life expectancy changes since the start of the pandemic, distinguishing countries that saw worsening losses from countries that managed to bounce back from their Life expectancy dropped in 2020.

Most countries experienced sizable gains in Life expectancy during the initial of the 20th century. However, at the turn of the twenty-first century, the rate of improvement in LE slowed in many high-income countries before the COVID-19 pandemic, such as the United States, England and Wales, and Scotland, among others. The COVID-19 crisis triggered a mortality shock resulting in Life expectancy declines in 2020 of a magnitude not observed in the recent history of high-income countries.

Fluctuations in Life expectancy are not uncommon. Typically, Life expectancy declines are quickly followed by bounce-backs. In contrast to these short-term fluctuations, however, the COVID-19 pandemic induced global and severe mortality shocks in 2020 and, as of spring 2022, is still ongoing. Throughout 2021, the impact of the pandemic became more heterogeneous across populations, with differences in prior infection, non-pharmaceutical interventions, and vaccination uptake, all influencing the pandemic's course.

Life expectancy is the specific years a newborn baby is predicted to live or the predicted number of years remaining for an individual of a certain age estimated from the death rates in a population. Examining mortality causes, patterns, and trends can also explain disparities and changes in health well-being, contribute to evaluating health programs and treatments, and drive planning and policymaking.

Longevity and Death

Longevity stems from the Latin word longaevitas, where longus means long, and aevum means age; the combination means "long age." People that live much longer than the average person could be said to have longevity. Therefore, longevity means long life.

Contrary to the statements of certain demographers and biologists, there may be no inherent limitation on the span of human existence, or at least one is not yet apparent.

According to Jean-Marie Robine, a demographer at France's National Institute of Health and Medical Research, there is no limit to human longevity if there is a mortality plateau.

Although many people live longer now than they would have lived in previous generations, the maximum human life span has remained roughly the same, about 120 years. This suggests a biologically determined limit beyond which human life cannot be extended, regardless of increased social support and healthcare progress. In other words, the extension of the human life span has been, and will probably continue to be, mainly horizontal rather than vertical. A crucial caveat acknowledged by prolongevitists is that one's quality of life in the years of extension not be reduced beyond what it would otherwise be. Quantity of life is good if and only if it entails qualitative satisfaction.

At an individual level, life expectancies at birth have increased globally from 47.9 years in the mid-20th century to around 70 years and are expected to rise to 76 years by the mid-21st century. At the population level, the percentage of the world's population aged 60 years and above has risen from 8 percent in the mid-20th century to 11 percent. By 2050, it is expected to reach 21 percent, equating to more than 2 billion people.

Globally, human longevity continues to increase. Focusing on maternity care, labor and delivery, childhood vaccines, smoking cessation, and healthier lives in terms of nutrition and exercise have significantly impacted human life duration worldwide. Intriguingly, one unique number stands out from the general trend: the disparity in human longevity between men and women. On average, men live shorter lifetimes than women around the world. An estimated 79.3 years is the typical American lifespan (World Health Organization [WHO], 2016). When this data is broken down by gender, women live an average of 81.6 years, while males just 76.9, a difference of 4.7 years. Table 65.1 displays global data on life expectancy, illustrating the disparity between male and female lifespans.

The gap exists across the globe and all strata of industrial development; Eastern Europe demonstrates the largest gap, approximately seven years. Even in sub-Saharan Africa, the region with the shortest life expectancy in the world, men live on average 5.3 years less than women. There is not one part of the world where men, on average, outlive women.

Longevity has evolved as a byproduct of genes selected for their contribution to the organism's ability to live till reproductive age. As a result, genetic determinism is a suitable underlying assumption for study designs investigating nutritional aspects associated with longevity. Aging is not the result of evolution but rather the result of stochastic and random events that most likely begin during the reproductively active years of early adulthood.

The genetic determinism approach, which compares young (normal, control) and old (abnormal, experimental) populations, need to be more effective in finding the underlying mechanisms and nutritional factors that influence aging. The objective of this book is to highlight briefly the distinction between aging and longevity, as well as why understanding this distinction is crucial for nutrition research and developing the most exact dietary recommendations for the elderly population.

The ability to define aging and longevity separately has become possible only in recent years. Biogerontological research conducted during the last two decades has, to a large degree, solved the evolutionary problem of longevity and aging. Evolutionary theorists have mathematically and empirically demonstrated that longevity is genetically determined from genes selected for reproductive advantage. Longevity did not consider the possibility that life span and the functional loss characterizing aging could have arisen through different evolutionary/biological processes. Subsequent work found that longevity and aging are different biological events.

While longevity is usually mistaken for life expectancy, the term usually refers to a specific long-lived population. These are people who live past their life expectancy. Life expectancy is the estimated number of years that an individual may live. When individuals live past this age, they are known to have longevity.

Chapter Two
Healthy Life Expectancy

Good health is the most important outcome of health care. Healthy life expectancy (HLE), an intuitive and meaningful summary measure combining the length and quality of life, has become a standard worldwide for measuring population health.

Healthy life expectancy (HLE) measures population health that combines life span and quality into a single metric. This book argues for the nationwide adoption of HLE as an outcome measure in the United States of America at the national, state, community, and healthcare system levels to compare the effectiveness of alternative practices, evaluate disparities, and guide resource allocation. We define healthcare systems broadly to include those organizations responsible for financing and delivering healthcare to a defined population. Although hospitals and physicians' groups without a defined population cannot measure HLE independently, they can contribute significant mortality and health status information to its calculation.

Health status indicators range from objective measures of physiologic, disease, and functional status (such as the ability to climb a flight of stairs) to subjective measures of self-perceived health. They also extend from single-question, global assessments of overall health status to assessments across multiple health domains, including physical and mental health and functional status.

HLE has two different and important interpretations. It is a valuable stand-alone measure of population health and is expressed as a percentage of overall life expectancy (LE).

However, measurements across various health and function areas provide a more comprehensive health assessment for people and societies. By splitting life expectancy into time spent in different health states, the healthy life expectancy metric adds a 'quality of life component to life expectancy calculations. The duration of years spent in poor health is particularly significant since it correlates more closely with the demand for health and social care and the associated costs.

Measuring the value of remaining years has been increasingly popular in recent years. Life expectancy has been frequently utilized as a measure of health. Health expectancy combines data on mortality and morbidity or disability; as a result, it provides an estimate of the remaining years predicted to be spent in good states of health or without disability. Health expectancy indicators have been widely used to compare various groups' health, track temporal trends, and investigate population health disparities.

The ability to handle a large of HIV, tuberculosis and malaria control measures beginning in 2005 has all contributed to the improvement in healthy life expectancy through increased access to essential health services, better reproductive, maternal, newborn, and child health, and more effective disease prevention and treatment. The average coverage for critical health services increased to 46% in 2019 from 24% in 2000. The most notable accomplishments were preventing and treating infectious diseases, countered by the huge increase in cases of hypertension, diabetes, and other noncommunicable diseases, and the failure to provide adequate health services to prevent and treat them. Unless robust catch-up preparations are implemented, the impact of the COVID-19 pandemic may also impede progress in healthy life expectancy. On average, African nations reported more disruptions to vital services than nations in other areas. More than ninety percent of the 36 nations that responded to a WHO poll in 2021 reported disruptions to vital health services, with immunization, neglected tropical diseases, and nutrition services suffering the most.

While death is retreating to increasingly higher ages, it is unclear whether the onset of disease and disability are doing the same, an issue that could endanger the proper functioning of contemporary societies (e.g., by threatening the sustainability of pension systems, or the provision of health care to increasingly older populations). The so-called "compression vs. expansion of morbidity" debate, which tries to elucidate whether morbidity retreats to older ages at a higher or lower speed than mortality does (5–7), has been raging for a long time. So far, the evidence supporting the different hypotheses is mixed, as the extent to which HLE compares with LE trends depends on the morbidity measures used to calculate HLE and country and time contexts.

Fertility rates have decreased gradually over the previous two decades, while life expectancy has increased with few exceptions. This transformation results from historical relationships between social and economic variables, such as those described by the GBD Socio-demographic Index and demographic results. Several countries have recently seen a mix of low fertility and stagnant progress in death rates, driving more people towards the last stages of demographic transition. It will be vital for global health monitoring to track demographic shifts and the emergence of new patterns.

Those residing in disadvantaged areas have a significantly lower Life Expectancy and Healthy Life Expectancy than those in less deprived areas. In most situations, the inequality gap has widened over the past decade.

Healthy Life Expectancy is a single measure of a population's health that considers the population's health condition and death rates at various ages. HLE can examine health trends over time and compare the health of various populations and subpopulations. It is useful for resource allocation, health and other services planning, and health result evaluation.

While one objective is to maximize the population's Life Expectancy, another is to maximize the population's Healthy Life Expectancy. In other words, the objective is a healthy life, not merely longevity. The difference between LE and HLE shows the length of time the average individual is anticipated to spend in "not healthy" health; consequently, while analyzing temporal trends, a third objective is to increase HLE so that it approaches LE, so lowering the gap or period of morbidity (ill-health). The proportion of the average lifespan projected to be spent in 'healthy' health (HLE/LE) is commonly used to evaluate whether morbidity is compressing (proportion increasing, i.e., less time spent in poor health) or an expansion of morbidity (proportion decreasing, i.e., more time spent in poor health) over time (proportion decreasing, i.e., more time spent in poor health).

However, both Life Expectancy and Healthy Life Expectancy are averages; thus, some people may have "not healthy" health in their early years even though most people will experience this state towards the end of their lives.

Life Expectancy and Healthy Life Expectancy are usually estimated for males and females separately, as, in Western Europe, women generally outlive men by several years.

The Average Number of Years Expected Of an Individual to Live In Good and Bad Health

Dr. Frank Hu, Harvard T.H. Chan School of Public Health chairman of the department of nutrition and senior author of the paper, explains, "It's essential to look at disease-free life expectancy because it has significant implications for enhancing life quality and reducing total health care costs." "Extending lifespan alone is insufficient; we also need to expand health span so that the extended life expectancy is long and healthy, with no significant chronic diseases and the associated limitations."

To determine these tendencies, researchers evaluated data obtained from more than 111,000 U.S. women and men between the ages of 30 and 75 who enrolled in the Nurses Health Study or the Health Professionals Follow-Up Study between 1980 and 1986. Through 2014, members filled out questionnaires every two years regarding their lifestyle and health. Each participant was assigned a "lifestyle" score between 0 and 5 based on their responses, with higher scores indicating greater adherence to health recommendations. The researchers attempted to establish a correlation between these scores and the length of time people were free of heart disease, cancer, and diabetes.

This is bad news for us, our health services, and the government. Therefore, we must adopt a healthier lifestyle and encourage the government and businesses to make healthy options more accessible to the general public.

The desire for a long and healthy life is frequently expressed. Nevertheless, not everyone will lead such a life. Life expectancy and healthy life expectancy disparities between groups remain significant. Many people will have subjective expectations regarding their life expectancy and future health-related quality of life, which may (significantly) differ from realistic forecasts. Such subjective expectations remain understudied, particularly regarding future health-related quality of life, although they may be significant for various reasons.

First, subjective expectations regarding life expectancy and future health-related quality of life may be significant if they influence decision-making. If individuals have particular views about how they will age and at what age they will reach old age, this may influence their current decisions in various life areas. For instance, expectations may influence the decision to invest in future health and longevity and pension and savings decisions. Therefore, understanding subjective expectations enable us to gain insight into and affect decision-making. Given the preventable death and morbidity linked to changeable, bad health behaviors, this is significant for the health domain.

People who anticipate that old age will be associated with a poor quality of life regardless of their current investments may be less motivated to take preventative measures. Moreover, persons who anticipate that aging will be connected with inevitable health decline may be less likely to utilize healthcare. For instance, Sarkisian et al. discovered that older persons with low expectations towards aging considered that accessing healthcare for age-related, controllable ill-health disorders was less significant. Consequently, subjective expectations on the length and quality of future life can impact current decisions. Especially when subjective expectations are wrong (such as being excessively gloomy), this might lead to suboptimal decisions.

Secondly, subjective expectations regarding length and future health-related quality of life may also play a role in research. For instance, in explaining discount rates observed in experiments or when valuing health states using the time trade-off (TTO) method, humans worldwide are living longer. Although there have been clear ups and downs, life expectancy at birth has been rising continuously for decades. It has increased by more than twofold in the last two centuries.

Previously, decreases in infant mortality drove this increase. Since the 1950s, however, the primary factor has been the decline in mortality among the elderly. In Sweden, where high-quality national population records have been recorded since the mid-16th century, the maximum lifetime has increased by nearly 150 years. A rising life expectancy has been recorded in numerous other nations, including Western Europe, North America, and Japan.

Humans around the world are living longer. Although there have been clear ups and downs, life expectancy at birth has been rising continuously for decades. It has increased by more than twofold in the last two centuries.

Longevity presents chances not only for the elderly and their families but also for society as a whole. Additional years allow for pursuing new endeavors, such as higher education, a new career, or a long-neglected interest. Additionally, older individuals contribute in numerous ways to their families and communities. Nonetheless, the magnitude of these opportunities and contributions highly depends on one factor: health.

Chapter Three
Women's Lifespans

A boy asked his father a philosophical question that left his father stunned and speechless. He said, "Dad, why do mummies live longer than Daddies?"

I know most of us have this thought ruminating in our minds, too. Don't worry; this chapter will answer all the questions.

On a global scale, women live longer than males, and scientists have linked the sex variations in longevity to a biological basis for survival. A new study of mammalian species in the field has uncovered significant disparities in life span and aging between mammalian species.

In humans, the average life duration of women is over 8% longer than men's. In contrast, females in 60% of the examined species of wild animals have, on average, 18.6% longer lifespans. The ratio varies significantly between various animal families.

The degree of the difference in a lifetime may also be influenced by local environmental conditions, which include a tradeoff between reproduction and survival. In certain animals, men devote more of their resources to sexual rivalry and reproduction, which, according to scientists, could result in greater sex inequalities in lifespans.

Another possible reason for the disparity between the sexes is that female survival is enhanced when males give some or all parental care. Giving birth and caring for the young is a huge health expense for females; thus, if both parents work jointly to raise their children, this cost is lowered.

The average American man will live to the age of 76, while the average American woman will live to the age of 81, according to the

U.S. Centers for Disease Control and Prevention. In their older years, women can also anticipate greater health than men. According to experts, the divide results from biological and social inequalities.

As men age, the testosterone hormone is associated with a decline in their immune system and an increased risk of cardiovascular disease. It is also associated with dangerous behaviors, such as smoking, drinking, and poor eating. Men are less likely than women to follow a doctor's recommendations if they are diagnosed. Men are statistically more prone to take life-threatening risks and die in automobile accidents or gun battles.

Currently, people live longer than they did in the past. But due to behavioral, biological, and other factors, life expectancy advances only benefit some equally.

Women outlive men in nearly all societies. In more industrialized nations, the average life expectancy at birth for women is 79 years, and for males, it is 72 years. In less developed nations, where high maternal mortality reduces the lifespan gap, women can expect to survive an average of 66 years, while men can expect to live an average of 63 years.

Males outlive women in only a few Asian and Southern African nations (Afghanistan, Nepal, Papua-New Guinea, Namibia, and Zimbabwe). Due to the rise in male mortality rates across the majority of the last four decades, Russia has the greatest female advantage, 13 years.

The disparity in life expectancy has not always been as significant as it is now. The NBER (National Bureau of Economic Research) survey reported that women did not regularly live longer than men until the onset of the 20th century, based on detailed mortality records. Before that time, infectious diseases were common and affected both genders somewhat equally. Moreover, women frequently die during childbirth.

Since then, the life expectancy of women has sometimes increased as rapidly as it could have. According to a 2011 report by the National Research Council, beginning in the mid-1970s, the disparity between potential and observed life expectancy for women began to expand. By 2005, on average, women were living 2,3 years shorter than projected because so many women had begun smoking.

Longstanding biological differences between women and men might produce a relatively rapid emergence of sex mortality differential only by interaction with relatively new exogenous environmental factors. The vast majority of studies on the sex differential in mortality trends confirm the importance of smoking as a major contributor to higher mortality in men than in women.

Along this line, other behavioral factors also influence longevity in women. With ongoing changes in society, especially the increasing participation of women in the labor force, new components of the environmental setting will have to be assessed by comparable and identical instruments in different populations. Ongoing monitoring of cardiovascular and noncommunicable disease trends will provide valuable insight into the sex mortality differential and its determinants. Experimental studies on biological reactivity, sex endocrinology, and atherogenesis are also needed to help explain why women live longer than men.

In contrast to biblical times, when men lived to be hundreds of years old while women lagged far behind in biological age, the tables have now been reversed, and men now trail women.

Women are the life-expectancy champions: Today, they can expect to live longer than men almost anywhere in the world. This pervasive inequality has intrigued researchers for decades. The cumulative corpus of research supports the conclusion that the gap has biological underpinnings modulated by social and environmental conditions. A deeper understanding could benefit from biodemographic research. Here we present some results of such a study.

Support for a biological root of the gender gap in survival stems from studies of groups in which men and women have more similar lifestyles than in the general population, such as among nonsmokers or within religious groups such as active Mormons or cloistered monks and nuns. Findings indicate that even though men and women in these groups have more similar lifestyles and women are exposed to fewer risk factors than men in the general population, a gender gap in life expectancy persists.

An untapped source of information is the reverse situation when both men and women experience high, perhaps extreme, levels of mortality risk. A finding that men and women have similar life expectancies under these conditions would challenge the notion that the survival advantage of women is fundamentally biologically determined in all environments. Therefore, we study the survival of both sexes in populations enduring mortality crises.

While women have lower mortality than men in modern populations, there is sparse evidence for a female survival advantage under crisis conditions.

Men had equal or higher mortality in all populations than women across almost all ages.

Medical Approach to Women's Lifespans

It is no secret that women's health needs and outcomes differ from men's. This is due to biological, environmental, and sociocultural factors. Differences in physiology, behavior, disease risk, symptom presentation, and drug metabolism influence women's health across the lifespan. These differences have been increasingly recognized over the past two decades.

Female subjects have historically been excluded from biomedical and toxicology research. White men were considered the "norm," and women were thought to have confounding factors given their fluctuating hormone levels.

As such, the data, preferred treatment, and outcomes from white men were then universally applied to all minorities and women as a standard regimen. There is no more precise illustration of this than studying cardiovascular disease in women. It is now well established that women have different symptoms and presenting features of an acute cardiovascular event than men. However, heart disease is the most common leading cause of death among American women. It was recognized in the early 2000s that only one-third of subjects for cardiovascular clinical trials were women, and 70% of these clinical trials did not report results according to sex. Although there have been improvements in women enrolled in clinical trials, numbers have remained low in some areas. This is believed to be related to low referral of women from their physicians and an inability to commit to the time required for study participation. Similar results have been discovered in a study on Alzheimer's disease, mental health syndromes, and certain types of cancers.

In addition, pregnant, lactating, and even women of "reproductive age" have been excluded from participating in clinical trials and labeled as vulnerable populations. This has resulted in much of the research on pregnant and lactating women being left to animal studies and retrospective data. It has been argued that the label "vulnerable populations" should be removed as this is defined as one whose "capacity to protect [its] interests and provide informed consent is undermined." As this definition does not describe most pregnant women, the recommendation is to label pregnant women, perhaps lactating women, as "scientifically complex." Gathering outcomes on pregnant and lactating women is important in ensuring appropriate treatment for all reproductive-age women.

It is also essential to address the differences between men and women beyond the biological level. Women face different experiences and expectations from societal and cultural norms. Cultural expectations can also affect health due to gender norms, health perceptions and misconceptions, and diet and food preferences.

Women often outlive males, which has been the case since the pre-industrial era. This is due to smaller bodies (and thus less anxiety on the heart), a stronger immune system (since testosterone serves as an immunosuppressant), and a decreased propensity to engage in physically hazardous activities to care for their grandkids and great-grandchildren. It is thought that women have an evolutionary advantage in living longer lives.

Education, work prospects, lifestyle practices, social mobility, and the broader local environment significantly impact male and female longevity. It appears that where we live influences how long we might live. However, regardless of where we reside, we may take steps to increase our likelihood of living a longer and healthier life. Many believe men live shorter lives because they smoke and perform harder jobs, but genetic and biochemical differences exist.

For instance, observe the blood of healthy individuals between the ages of 65 and 95. Sex may potentially affect a person's prognosis after being diagnosed with Covid-19, the novel coronavirus disease.

A recent study discovered that men lose antibody-producing B cells in their blood after age 65, although women do not experience the same loss. The researchers also discovered that as men aged, their blood inflammation increased, a condition related to severe cases of Covid-19.

Nevertheless, women do not have every biological advantage. According to research, women suffer a spike in blood pressure earlier and more rapidly than males.

It was assumed that women had caught up to males regarding cardiovascular risk, not that their biology and physiology varied.

In addition, female hormones and women's reproductive roles have been related to increased longevity.

As they live longer, more women are at risk for chronic diseases such as cardiovascular illness, cancer, stroke, and Alzheimer's. However, there is also good news. Because of preventative measures and new, more effective therapies for diseases, women are living longer.

Chapter Four

Men's Lifespan

Women outliving men in today's population is nothing new. Some studies concentrate on the biological causes of female advantage, while others emphasize the importance of social influences. We looked at differences in male and female survival in slave groups and populations that had experienced severe famines and epidemics. Women, on average, lived longer than men, even in periods of exceptionally high mortality. Baby girls were better able to withstand harsh environments than baby boys, accounting for most female advantages. The results line up with the theory that a complex interplay between biological, environmental, and social factors controls the female survival advantage.

When social circumstances may be neutral or favor male survival, behavioral differences are unlikely to play a substantial influence. The condition where mortality risk is high, possibly very high, for both men and women represents a new supply of knowledge. The idea that women have a fundamental biological advantage in terms of survival in all contexts would be challenged if it were shown that men and women have similar life expectancies under these circumstances. As a result, in this research, we examine the survival of both sexes in communities experiencing mortality crises.

While women have lower mortality than men in modern populations, there is sparse evidence for a female survival advantage under crisis conditions. A well-known story concerns the Donner Party, a group of settlers that lost twice as many men as women when stranded for six months in the extreme winter in the Sierra Nevada Mountains.

The fact that men's estrogen levels are lower than women's could contribute to this. Medical hazards, however, such as untreated high blood pressure or unhealthy cholesterol levels, may also be a factor. To be bigger than females. Larger animals typically outlive smaller ones across many species.

Women generally outlive men worldwide, and male mortality is higher for almost all major causes of death. Many other mammal species, including humans, also exhibit a female advantage in longevity.

Men typically die younger in developed countries due to their higher risk of unhealthy behaviors. Males have a greater fatality rate from lung cancer, accidents, suicide, and homicide due to their higher rates of cigarette smoking, heavy drinking, gun use, employment in hazardous occupations, and risk-taking during recreation and driving.

In underdeveloped nations, men experience greater death rates due to their riskier habits, but this gender disparity has been less pronounced than in industrialized nations. Both sexes experience an increased mortality rate from infectious diseases due to environmental variables such as contaminated water and poor nutrition. However, there are added hazards for women when giving birth. Sub-Saharan Africa has a high maternal death rate, while China has a greater prevalence of female suicide than male suicide.

Men are more prone than women to suffer from hearing loss, circulatory issues like cardiovascular disease and diabetes, and smoking-related illnesses like emphysema and respiratory cancer.

However, women and men with identical chronic conditions rate their health similarly. Despite this, men with respiratory cancer, cardiovascular disease, and bronchitis have a higher mortality risk than women with these conditions. This suggests that men may experience more severe manifestations of these conditions.

Because women frequently have far lower social status than males in developing nations, the gender gap in mortality is also less in these nations. The gender gap is anticipated to widen in developing countries as women's standing catches up to men's. However, it is anticipated that when women adopt unhealthy behaviors like men—drinking more, smoking more, and being more stressed out at work—the gender gap will narrow in industrialized nations. Male risk-taking behavior may be influenced by both biology and culture. According to research, testosterone is partly responsible for men's higher levels of physical activity and aggression. This "domino effect" raises men's mortality rates from accidents and homicide. When examining gender inequalities in health and mortality, it can be difficult to discern biological differences. Ingrid Waldron, a biology professor at the University of Pennsylvania, asserts, "You can't disentangle the societal distinctions from the biology." They are sold as a set.

Low-wage or manual labor appears to be detrimental to health. People in the lowest income bracket have poorer health and a more rapid decline in health while employed. Even though manual laborers are, on average, less healthy than other occupations, the differences between male and female employees in this occupational group are far fewer than the differences between occupations.

Differences also influence variations in health-related behaviors in men's and women's behavioral expectations and instruction. Many societies, for instance, encourage or condone heavy drinking among men but condemn it among women. Also, in many cultures, women are not expected to participate in the monetary economy outside the home, whereas males are expected to be part of the labor force.

Because women are less likely to be employed than men, they are less susceptible to the adverse effects of employment. Consequently, their health declines less rapidly.

Changes over time can impact the disparity between life expectancies. In most developed nations, men's widespread adoption of cigarette smoking throughout the first half of the 20th century significantly contributed to the expanding mortality gap between the sexes. Later, the mortality disparity narrowed in the United States as women began to smoke more and men began to smoke less.

The average male lifespan is five years less than that of females. Additionally, men are two to four times more likely to die prematurely from unintentional injury, homicide, and suicide than women. These figures are sad and result from numerous societal and biological factors. It's encouraging to know that many of these protective variables are modifiable, especially with regular preventative care.

Depression affects one in ten persons in the United States, and men are disproportionately affected by mental health concerns, particularly depression. Symptoms are not always visible, and in a culture where "suck it up" and "no pain, no gain" are prominent, symptoms are frequently overlooked. Depression is typically expressed differently by men and women. According to James Korman, PsyD, ACT, director of the Behavioral Health and Cognitive Therapy Center at Summit Medical Group in New Jersey, this can result in disturbed sleep, mood swings, and sexual apathy. Telling your doctor is the most crucial step you can take or your loved one if you believe you may be depressed.

Men are more prone than women to smoke more, consume too much alcohol, and overindulge in food. These behaviors increase the risk of developing diabetes, high cholesterol, obesity, and other conditions that decrease lifespan. If you smoke, give it up. It's the riskiest health behavior, regardless of age or gender. If you desire a milkshake or an additional pint of beer, that's fine; don't make it a habit. There's a reason why the adage "all things in moderation" exists: it's healthier for your health.

Men should check their egos at the door and schedule frequent medical examinations. Routine doctor checkups can detect health issues before they become permanent. Male patients need to discuss frankly with their physicians, as many of their "embarrassing" symptoms, such as erectile dysfunction, might be linked to more serious medical conditions, such as diabetes and cardiovascular disease. In addition, persons with improved health due to prevention are more productive and may earn a higher average income than adults with preventable/treatable diseases.

Men frequently tread a finer line between safety and danger than women. The proverb "drive fast, take chances" captures the social side of guys living dangerously. Men are more likely to drive recklessly and cause more car accidents than women. Want that fast car or motorcycle? It is acceptable if you are conscious of the risk of harm. Eliminate distractions while driving, including the use of cell phones, and concentrate on defensive driving techniques. In one study, even when used hands-free, cell phones were found to quadruple a man's risk of an accident.

Medical Approach to Men's Lifespan

Despite the higher death rate for men than women, this page will highlight a few safety measures.

Men in this age range are more likely to participate in dangerous behaviors, such as drinking and driving, because the brain doesn't reach complete maturation until the mid-20s.

It would help if you created healthy habits early in life to maintain them well into your 70s and beyond. Get the appropriate screenings from your doctor and take steps to avoid substance abuse, accidents, and sexually transmitted diseases that could have long-lasting effects. Additionally, you might want to create a baseline for indicators like blood pressure, diabetes, and thyroid disease.

Men in this age range (the 30s to 40s) sometimes work double shifts to juggle the responsibilities of jobs and family. Unfortunately, such an approach might not work. In addition to the adverse effects of not getting enough sleep, your body may also experience changes that make taking care of oneself even more crucial.

Men's metabolisms slow in their 30s and 40s. Consequently, even if you consume the same amount of food, you will probably gain more weight.

What you should do is: Men need to commit to caring for themselves. Eat well, obtain seven to nine hours of sleep each night, and exercise four to five times per week. Then undergo screening for conditions like thyroid illness, diabetes, and cardiovascular risk factors (including cholesterol levels and blood pressure).

After the age of 50, testosterone levels start to decline, which affects how fat is distributed. Men may notice that their belly is gaining extra weight, and their hair is growing more in their nose and ears and less on their head. Estrogen and estradiol levels may increase concurrently, altering breast tissue and depleting muscle mass. Additionally, their sexual function and desire may decline. When they are aware these changes are forthcoming, it's less alarming when they happen.

You should prioritize your heart and brain health, and if the sufferer smokes, arrange for a lung cancer screening (and do your best to kick the habit). Consult a doctor for assistance if the changes in your sexual function worry you. Men should be able to enjoy a healthy sex life well into their golden years because of the various treatments available.

Abusing substances can result in short-term, direct impacts as well as long-term, indirect repercussions. People who struggle with substance misuse may experience physical ailments, including irregular heartbeats. People who struggle with substance use disorders frequently experience chronic issues like heart and respiratory diseases.

Meanwhile, since 1999, the number of overdose deaths in the United States has more than tripled, with a disproportionately high percentage of men being responsible. The main chemicals implicated in these deaths were opioids, cocaine, and synthetic drugs.

Additionally, because substance misuse can result in shaky judgment and unsafe behaviors, it can indirectly impact health and longevity.

Adults need seven hours of good sleep each night, per the Mayo Clinic. A full night's sleep is crucial because it allows the body's immune system to repair and regenerate cells. The endocrine and digestive systems also use sleep to recover from damage.

These systems must function correctly to fight off diseases and provide natural energy during the day. Sleep can also affect cognitive abilities and mental health. As they age, men sacrifice sleep because of work and family duties.

Premature death can result directly or indirectly through reckless activity, such as driving too fast, not using a seatbelt, using drugs, or engaging in risky sex practices. Homicide, the second-leading cause of death for young males, can result from actively seeking out violence and carrying lethal weapons.

Men must practice fundamental safety procedures and avoid potentially dangerous situations to avoid unintentional injuries and preventable diseases and refrain from violence.

Chapter Five

Determinants of Children's Lifespan

In developing nations, where most infant and child deaths result from a string of episodes of infection combined with malnutrition rather than a single cause, a strategy focused on specific diseases will not be effective. Therefore, health programs must pinpoint the risk factors that lower survival chances and the diseases that result in mortality. Risk factors can be divided into two categories: *proximate determinants*, which are the fundamental biological processes that directly affect risks of morbidity and mortality, and *underlying determinants*, which are all the other social and environmental determinants that affect infant survival by acting indirectly through the proximate determinants. The first step in applying the focus on proximate determinants is to clearly understand some measurable biological indicators of health and child survival or their opposites, illness, and death. Abnormal growth is a sensitive and nonspecific indicator of morbidity in children.

Mortality and permanent growth stunting reflect different points of chronic and irreversible physical deterioration on the continuum that ranges from good health to death.

Age at first birth, area, domicile, education, wealth index, and the fathers' and mothers' religions were essential drivers of childhood mortality. Every unit increase in age was shown to increase the incidence of the outcome in the link between childhood mortality and the parents' ages. The opposite was true for age at first birth, which was likewise statistically significant. The study concludes that to achieve good life expectancy meetings, policymakers and stakeholders in health care should provide for improved living standards.

The probability of living to a ripe old age is transmitted from parents to offspring in a modest but robust manner. The inheritance of individual resilience parallels longevity inheritance. Individual resilience develops as a response to hardship and experience in general during the early stages of life. This results in a transgenerational trajectory that is separate from social class trajectories. A theory of longevity inheritance should incorporate new findings from epigenetics and social epidemiology with existing ideas of general vulnerability, frailty, and resistance.

Even with welfare state benefits, modern treatment, and a fundamental shift in the illness landscape, we continue to observe a negative social gradient in mortality. According to sociological studies, "the long shadow of the past" impacts succeeding generations' educational and professional paths, maintaining socio-economic (dis) advantages over time. We should anticipate that the parental generation's characteristics—education, occupation, and income—which all predict health and survival—will likewise predict the next generation's health prospects, leading to the "inheritance of longevity." However, this influence from previous generations may be considerably broader than that of working through the children's education, occupation, and income. Variation in mortality risk within social groups is great. To understand the "inheritance of longevity," we need a conceptual framework that identifies those within-class influences.

The so-called DOHaD (Developmental Origins of Health and Disease) theory suggests that early life experiences are an important determinant of adult health and disease (Gluckman, Hanson, Cooper, & Thornburg, 2008). DOHaD theory has focused on specific aetiologies and influences, such as fetal growth restriction on blood pressure and circulatory disease.

Demographic concepts like frailty, epidemiological ones like general susceptibility, and psychological ones like resilience all refer to the same real-life phenomenon: a general rather than specific vulnerability to disease.

Demographic concepts like frailty, epidemiological ones like general susceptibility, and psychological ones like resilience all refer to the same real-life phenomenon: a general rather than specific vulnerability to disease.

Consistent with that view, a Swedish study of men born in 1913 found that several social and behavioral factors measured at age 50, but not their parents' survival, predicted longevity.

Nevertheless, we observe a steady lifespan extension in modern societies, especially among women, partly based on falling mortality rates across their long post-reproductive period. That children tend to live longer than their parents are likely to be determined both by what experience parents bring to the next generation and by the improved life circumstances of the children themselves in their childhood and adult life. The importance of genetic factors for longevity lies in their interaction with other factors, especially if this interaction occurs at an early age. Evolutionary theorists have debated whether there is any evolutionary pressure to promote survival into old age.

The ability to survive into old age may be transmitted across generations. This inheritance cannot be reduced to the influence of parents' social class or marital status at the time of the child's birth to the birth order of the new individual or shared genes. In all social classes and family types, considerable individual heterogeneity exists in the ability to reach a high age. We propose that this heterogeneity, to some extent, mirrors a person's very early experience, such as her history of coping with challenging and adverse experiences early in life.

How the individual handles early experiences and whether or not she can rely on support from family and friends may be crucial for the differential adaption to adversity. Small initial differences in trajectories between children in similar family circumstances, even between siblings, may be reinforced and greatly magnified during development along a resilience/susceptibility dimension.

Firstly, parental care and understanding of how to cope with success and adversity. Secondly, specific "longevity genes" promote resilience and long life could be inherited in families. More intriguingly, the third is the possibility that resilience may be fixed in the germ line epigenome early in life.

Parents' survival to older ages and later deaths. The capacity to "bounce back" from the adversity of difficulty appears to be the idea's central tenet. A successful reaction to adversity can be learned early in life and is known as resilience.

It was recorded that continuity of resilience from fathers to sons, independent of parental social class. This characteristic could be transmitted across generations through several mechanisms (not mutually exclusive), such as learning from parents or transmitting specific genes. Of theoretical importance is the hypothesis that early experience can also cause epigenetic modification of germ-line DNA and potentially influence gene expression and longevity in the next generation.

Human resilience is shaped over time, including childhood and adolescence.

The longevity of parents indicates the long-term mortality of their offspring. Their parents' social class and marital status at the time of their birth have no bearing on this influence, and it is separate from their social class trajectories.

Answers to the Philosophical Questions about Longevity Heredity

Longevity in humans is grouped within particular families. Understanding this clustering is crucial, significantly advancing our knowledge of the genetic and environmental factors influencing longevity and healthy aging. Maternal or paternal effects determined whether parents lived long.

Longevity is transmitted even if parents don't know; it becomes longevous, which supports the notion that a beneficial genetic component was transmitted. Likewise, the identified associations are additive in that an increase in the number of parents, siblings, or aunts and uncles is associated with an increase in the survival of Identified Patients (IPs) and the children of IPs.

Human Lifespan (defined as age at death) has a low heritability in the population. Studies estimated the heritability of lifespan between 12% and 25%, and a recent study estimated that the heritability of lifespan was even lower, ~7%, after adjustment for the lifespans of nongenetic (in-law) relatives4. Therefore lifespan-based gene mapping may need to be more fruitful. In addition, the genetic component of lifespan includes the heritability of early life mortality, mainly due to disease and external causes. Despite the low heritability and polygenic architecture of lifespan, recent genetic studies have identified and replicated some lifespan loci of which the rare alleles lower the risk of age-related diseases. Hence, using the lifespan trait hampers the identification of genetic loci contributing to survival into extreme ages (longevity). Longevity, however, clusters strongly within families, as shown by previous studies and robustly quantified in this study.

Hence, the longevity trait is much more promising and appropriate for identifying genetic loci contributing to survival into extreme ages and should be distinct from the lifespan trait. The results imply that to find loci that promote survival to the highest ages in the population; genetic studies should be based on long-lived cases, including at least parental mortality information but preferably also mortality information of siblings and other first and second-degree relatives.

The longevity threshold should include cases belonging to the top 10% of survivors, with parents belonging to the top 15% of survivors of their birth cohort and siblings belonging to the top 10% of survivors of their birth cohort. To sharpen the longevity effect, the percentile threshold applied may be more extreme but would likely lead unnecessarily to a sample size with limited power. If our proposed longevity definition is consistently applied across studies, the comparative nature of longevity studies may improve and facilitate the discovery of novel genetic variants.

Survival to extreme age clusters within families. The atmosphere in which you grow up and your lifestyle choices also affect your life span. Some experts say the nature versus nurture argument is an oversimplification regarding longevity.

Research shows that certain activities and lifestyle choices can impact which DNA "switches" get turned on and off. One study trusted Source showed that mindfulness meditation practices could positively impact the genes related to inflammation and pain. Other research shows that gene expression can be altered by insufficient sleep.

While we can't control which genes we're born with, we can make healthy choices (like eating healthy foods, exercising regularly, avoiding smoking, and keeping up with doctor's appointments) throughout our lives that can improve our chances of living independently into our 90s, regardless of mom's life span, said Etingin.

The take-home message is that you can't do anything with a hand of cards you got dealt. Your genes are your genes, maybe one day we can change that, but right now, we cannot. Spend a lot of time on how you play that hand — that's the lifestyle you choose to live.

According to current estimates, genetics account for 25% of lifespan, with environmental influences and other factors accounting for 75%. A genetic study has significantly focused on understanding the biological processes influencing our longevity.

Family studies demonstrated that about 25 % of the variation in human longevity is due to genetic factors. The search for the genetic and molecular basis of aging has led to the identification of genes correlated with the maintenance of the cell and its basic metabolism as the main genetic factors affecting the individual variation of the aging phenotype. In addition, studies on calorie restriction and the variability of genes associated with nutrient-sensing signaling have shown that a hypocaloric diet and a genetically efficient metabolism of nutrients can modulate lifespan by promoting efficient maintenance of the cell and the organism. Recently, epigenetic studies have shown that epigenetic modifications, modulated by both genetic background and lifestyle, are very sensitive to the aging process and can either be a biomarker of the quality of aging or influence the rate and the quality of aging.

Chapter 6

Relationship between Lifespan and Genetics

Genetics, environment, and lifestyle all impact how long people live. With major increases in food and clean water availability, better housing and living circumstances, decreased exposure to infectious diseases, and more access to medical treatment, environmental changes starting in the 1900s dramatically increased the average life duration. The most important public health advancements lowered premature death by reducing the risk of infant mortality, increasing the likelihood of surviving childhood, and preventing infection and infectious disease. The average lifespan in the United States is approximately 80 years; however, some individuals live far longer.

The tendency for longer lifespans to run in families raises the possibility that shared genetics, lifestyle choices, or both significantly impact longevity.

The study of longevity genes is an emerging field of inquiry. An estimated 25 percent of the variation in human life span is attributed to genetics, but it is unclear which and how genes contribute to longevity. Some prevalent variations (known as polymorphisms) linked to longer life spans are present in the APOE, FOXO3, and CETP genes but not in all individuals with exceptional longevity. It is probable that variants in multiple genes, some unidentified, work in concert to contribute to a long life.

Many nonagenarians and centenarians can live independently and avoid age-related ailments until their final years. Scientists are examining people in their nineties (known as nonagenarians) and hundreds (known as centenarians, including semi-supercentenarians of ages 105-109 years and supercentenarians ages 110+) to identify what factors contribute to their long lives.

However, the supercentenarians also have numerous newly found gene variations that may increase longevity.

Some of the gene variants that contribute to a long life are engaged in the basic maintenance and function of the cells of the body. These biological tasks include DNA repair, maintenance of chromosome ends (regions known as telomeres), and protection of cells against harm caused by unstable oxygen-containing molecules (free radicals). Other genes associated with blood fat (lipid) levels, inflammation, and the cardiovascular and immune systems substantially reduce the risk of cardiovascular disease (the main cause of death in older persons), stroke, and insulin resistance.

In addition to studying the elderly in the United States, scientists are examining a few towns in Japan, Greece, and Italy where individuals frequently live into their nineties and beyond: Okinawa, Ikaria, and Sardinia (Italy). These three regions are similar in that they are somewhat isolated from most people in their respective countries, have lower incomes, less industrialization, and have a traditional (non-Western) way of life. In contrast to other groups of the very elderly, many Sardinian centenarians are male. On this island, researchers are investigating whether hormones, sex-specific genes, or other variables contribute to longer lives in both men and women.

However, about 40% of human life expectancy is inherited among generations, and many lifespan-associated genes are genetic. The study has included more than fifty genes reported in the literature for their contributions to the longevity of life. Intact genomic DNA is essential for cell, tissue, and organ life activities.

Nucleic acids are vulnerable to oxidative stress, chemotherapies, and radiation exposure. Efficient DNA repair mechanisms are essential for the maintenance of genomic integrity; damaged DNA is not replicated and transferred to the next generations; rather, the presence of harmful DNA initiates signaling cascades leading to cell cycle arrest or apoptosis. DNA modifications, DNA methylation, histone methylation, histone acetylation, and DNA damage can eventually lead to apoptosis. It has also been discussed how crucial calorie restriction therapy is for extending longevity. Additionally, the function of pathways, including DAF-16/FOXO (forkhead box protein O1), TOR, and JNK pathways involved in controlling lifespan, has been emphasized. The study shows the genetic factors linked to a longer lifespan and how they interact with cellular pathways to contribute to those factors.

Human genes and their orthologs are connected to lifespan longevity. The primary physiological functions and known associations with fatal disorders have been discussed for each gene.

Cell cycle regulating protein, encoded by the gene p53, is in charge of preserving the stability of the genome, lowering the rate of mutation, and suppressing cancer. P53 mutations have been regularly associated with human malignancies; this gene is disrupted in roughly 50% of all tumors. The fact that the p53 gene is present in organisms with short lifespans—such as worms and flies—that don't get cancer suggests that the gene has more uses than just tumor suppression. The presence of the p53 gene in short-lived organisms such as worms and flies, which do not develop cancers, indicates that tumor suppression is not the only function of the p53 gene. According to recent studies, p53 and p73 play crucial roles in reproduction.

Both longevity of lifespan and maturity age for reproduction are always coupled.

Sirtuin (SIRT) is thought to play a key role in extending lifespan by postponing cellular senescence. Sirtuin enhances DNA repair, which increases cellular capacity to maintain genome integrity. It can improve a cellular system's capacity and increase its resistance to oxidative stress.

Living things have extremely flexible lifespans that are susceptible to internal physiological and environmental factors that control epigenetics.

Expression and suppression levels of tens and hundreds of genes have significantly contributed to life's expected longevity. We have tabulated genes, and a few have been elaborated for their influence on regulating the aging process and lifespan. However, these pathways shift to protective and stress-bearing modes under adverse conditions, eventually leading to an extended lifespan.

There is enough information and a variety of supporting evidence to show that DNA damage plays a significant role in life extension and the contribution made by gene expression control systems.

Disentangling the causes of the human lifespan, a complicated feature, will have significant theoretical and clinical implications for biomedicine. Despite several studies using various methodologies and techniques, the genetics of the human lifespan still needs to be better understood. Here, the extraordinarily complex human lifespan phenotype is substantially to blame for such a relatively underwhelming harvest. An unusual confluence of gene-environment interactions is the cause of the capacity to live into the extreme decades of the human lifespan.

Consequently, the genetics of human longevity is explained here as a highly context-dependent phenomenon, within a novel integrated, ecological, and evolutionary viewpoint, and as a historically and individually dynamic process. The available literature has been analyzed from this perspective, paying particular attention to aspects largely overlooked (such as gender, individual biography, family, population ancestry, social structure, economic status, and education).

Homo sapiens is a long-lived mammal that likely acquired unique strategies for longevity. A higher level of complexity characterizes modern humans due to their biological and cultural capacities to adapt to all regions of the world and alter their environments due to the development of an extraordinarily diverse array of adaptive cultural techniques. This particular trait had and continues to significantly impact the molecular and cellular mechanisms involved in aging and longevity. Consequently, the genetics of human longevity is presented as a highly context-dependent phenomenon within a new integrated, ecological, and evolutionary framework and as a historically and individually dynamic process.

A challenging problem in the study of the genetics of lifespan is how to define controls. It's noteworthy that the studies can be split into two primary categories: (1) Research including younger, healthy controls from the same family or the broader community; (2) Research involving patients with age-related illnesses, presuming that these illnesses, as recently claimed, constitute a condition of accelerated aging. 4 The new era of molecular biomarkers of aging, which introduce the idea of biological age, is also leading to the emergence of a new definition of controls (described in the section Perspectives).

The genetic identity of each human is a dynamic process since each person has a unique genetic composition with a unique blend of common and rare or even private de novo variants (germline variations). At the same time, the accumulation of somatic mutations is noticed throughout the age. The combinations of these genetic variants comprise an individual's continuously evolving genetic identity.

Studying uncommon variations in aging and longevity is difficult since longevity is a rare characteristic.

Lifespan runs in families is a statement that introduces the great majority of publications on the genetics of human longevity, and families are an ecological niche. One of the earliest pieces of evidence was derived from geographical-genealogical investigations of the Sardinian population (Italy).

The Connection between Parental Lifespan and Children's Ageing

Numerous men and women frequently ponder the best time to start a family. Concerns concerning the impact of fertility postponement on offspring are growing as parental ages at birth continue to rise. Advanced parental ages have been linked to poor health outcomes for offspring, including shorter lifespans resulting from reproductive aging.

When cohort improvements in mortality are considered, we discover that children born to older mothers do not have any real mortality disadvantages and that children born to older fathers experience lower mortality. These results are probably explained by secular mortality declines offsetting the detrimental effects of reproductive aging.

When analyzing the association between parental age at childbearing and offspring health and longevity, there are at least three significant factors to consider: physiological effects, socio-economic position, and macro-level patterns in mortality. Each of these is discussed in turn.

The first factor is the physiological influence of parental age on offspring health, which is caused by reproductive aging. As humans age, their reproductive systems weaken. Increasing maternal age is connected with a buildup of DNA damage in the germ cells and a decline in embryo viability, resulting in decreased fertility.

Studies indicate that the risk of spontaneous abortion, stillbirth, and Down syndrome, as well as the risk of poor perinatal outcomes such as pre-term birth and low birth weight, increases exponentially for potential moms aged 25 and older. Additionally, children of older moms have a higher risk of acquiring childhood malignancies. The age of the father is also significant. Increasing father age is a key predictor of de novo mutations in male germ cells, and later paternal age has been linked to increased chances of schizophrenia and autism. The offspring of older parents experience increased mortality and reduced reproductive fitness in maturity, and the offspring of older mothers are particularly less likely to live to be centenarians, according to research. In addition, those born to older parents have an increased risk of developing Alzheimer's disease or schizophrenia as adults.

The parental socio-economic position is the second factor that affects the link between parental age at childbirth and offspring longevity. Older moms of the same cohort often have better levels of education, higher salaries, and higher occupational position. They frequently partner with men with high socioeconomic status due to assortative mating. According to studies, older couples are happier after having children and are more likely to be in stable relationships than younger ones. Most men and women from less privileged socio-economic backgrounds have children in their teens or as young adults. Even when this is not the case, childbearing at relatively young ages tends to be associated with lower mental and physical health levels. It disrupts educational and occupational trajectories, leading to lower socio-economic attainment and worse health for those parents. As a consequence, the children of older parents are generally the beneficiaries of greater resources and higher parenting quality.

Macro-level patterns in mortality are a crucial third element in determining the longevity of children by parental age at the time of delivery. Any prospective parent who delays parenthood will have their child born later. Only recently, individuals conducting a study on this topic disregarded the conceptual significance of this aspect. Recent research that explicitly considered the importance of cohort improvements over time demonstrates that, on average, the offspring of older mothers have a higher IQ, attain a higher level of schooling, and are taller. These benefits are attributed to rising IQ scores at the population level, the spread of education, and the continuous growth in population height. This is likely to also apply to child longevity, with those born to older parents benefiting from placement in a later birth cohort, given the secular declines in mortality.

In general, parents live longer than people without children. For adoptive parents, the effect is very pronounced: adopting one child extends lifespan by three years, and adopting two or three children extends lifespan by five years.

Chapter Seven

Life Expectancy in the United States

Life expectancy isn't truly a forecast for one specific person. It serves as a more accurate barometer of the state of society as a whole than a check engine light. Life expectancy will decrease if there are more deaths than would be anticipated or if they occur at younger ages than would be expected.

The United States life expectancy at birth dropped to 76.1 years, marking the most significant two-year dip in a century and the lowest level since 1996.

Life expectancy has increased significantly in the United States and other comparable nations during the past few decades. Life expectancy has generally grown as healthcare has advanced and more people have access.

Since the 1980s, however, the United States' growth in life expectancy at birth has deviated from that of comparable nations. Life expectancy in the U.S. has risen by around three fewer years than in peer nations between 1980 and 2019.

Compared to most other countries, the COVID-19 pandemic has increased mortality and early death rates in the U.S. Life expectancy isn't truly a forecast for one specific person. It serves as a more accurate barometer of the state of society as a whole than a check engine light. Life expectancy will decrease if there are more deaths than would be anticipated or if they occur at younger ages than would be expected. Peer nations. According to preliminary projections for life expectancy in 2020, the pandemic may have widened the difference in life expectancy between the United States and peer nations.

Racial differences in COVID-19 mortality contributed to the more significant decline in U.S. life expectancy compared to other nations. According to preliminary CDC statistics, In 2020, life expectancy at birth decreased across all races and ethnicities in the United States. However, life expectancy at birth declined more for non-Hispanic Black and Hispanic individuals than for non-Hispanic White people (-2.9 years and -3 years, respectively) (-1.2 years). The reduction in life expectancy among non-Hispanic Whites in the United States was more than the average decline in comparable nations (-1.2 years vs. -0.5 years).

Since 1980, the inequalities in life expectancy between men and women have decreased on average in the United States and comparable countries. In recent years, however, the life expectancy gap between men and women in the United States has been slowly widening. The disparity in life expectancy between women and men in comparable countries was previously greater than in the United States. However, in 2013, the United States surpassed comparable nations in this category. In 2019, the life expectancy gap between men and women in the United States was 5.1 years and 4.4 years in comparable nations. Due to COVID-19, the difference in life expectancy between men and women in the United States will increase to 5.4 years by 2020.

Since 1980, the average disparity in life expectancy between men and women in the United States and other comparable nations has shrunk. However, the discrepancy in life expectancy between American men and women has been gradually widening in recent years. For a while, comparable nations' disparities in life expectancy between men and women were greater than those of the United States. However, starting in 2013, the United States has overtaken them in this measure. In the United States, the difference in life expectancy between men and women as of 2019 was 5.1 years, compared to 4.4 years in comparable nations. Due to COVID-19, the difference in life expectancy between men and women in the U.S. increased to 5.4 years in 2020.

In 1980, the United States life expectancy and healthcare spending per capita was comparable to those in comparative nations.

In recent years, however, healthcare spending other the U.S. has increased faster than in peer nations, but life expectancy has increased more slowly. In 2019, the United States, which significantly outspent its neighbors, had the lowest life expectancy, while Japan, which spent the second least, had the greatest.

Other high-income countries have seen a rise in life expectancy, making the United States' results "all the more tragic," according to Woolf.

American Indian and Alaska Native people will experience one of the most dramatic drops in life expectancy in 2021.

The population's life expectancy is projected to drop to 65.2 from 70.2 in 2019.

"That's awful," Woolf exclaims. "The COVID-19 pandemic has caused horrific losses in the Native American population. And it illustrates many obstacles native populations must overcome to obtain healthcare, according to him.

According to Elizabeth Aria of the CDC's National Center for Health Statistics, who served as the report's primary author, the life expectancy for this community is currently the same as it was for the entire population in the 1940s.

According to Chandos Colleen, director of federal relations for the National Council of Urban Indian Health, American Indians have a 2.2 times higher risk of dying from COVID-19 and a 3.2 times higher risk of being hospitalized for the virus, despite a high vaccination uptake in this community. You'll see these numbers, and "it breaks your heart," he says.

White Americans experienced a greater decline in life expectancy than Black and Hispanic Americans in 2021. This was the opposite of what occurred in 2020 when Hispanic Americans experienced a four-year fall and Black Americans experienced a three-year decline. In 2021, the life expectancy of white Americans decreased by one year to 76.4 years. Black Americans saw a decrease of 0.7 years to 70.8 years, while Hispanic Americans saw a decrease of 0.2 years to 77.7 years. Asian Americans' life expectancy decreased by 0.1 years to 83.5 years.

The disparity in life expectancy between the United States and other nations has been expanding for decades. In addressing concerns like heart disease, the top cause of mortality in the country, the United States has lagged behind other nations.

In 2015, life expectancy declined for the first time since 1993, with some groups experiencing bigger declines than others. Inequality in life expectancy has ceased decreasing and is increasing along several dimensions, such as between Americans with low and high incomes. Analyses of mortality statistics from 1950 to 2015 provide context for recent developments, demonstrate that life expectancy and inequality in life expectancy are typically inversely connected, and propose policy reforms that could reduce disparities in life expectancy and help people live longer.

Changes in the mortality rate at the 20th percentile should be of interest to all those concerned with income-, education-, race-, and genetic disorder-related disparity. There can be a little assumption that the poor, the school dropouts, the victims of discrimination, and the unlucky genetic endowment causes a disproportionate number of premature deaths. Increased life expectancy and reduced inequality are major health policy objectives.

A newborn born in the United States in 2016 can expect to live an average of 78.6 years, a decrease from 78.9 years in 2014. 1993 was the last time life expectancy was lower than the previous year. 1962-63 was the last time it fell for two consecutive years.

Current attempts to improve survival and most research funded by the National Institutes of Health are disproportionately weighted toward combating heart disease and cancer, the primary causes of death and the ailments older Americans experience most frequently. By allocating greater resources to preventing the murderers of our youth, such as suicide, firearms, and accidents, particularly motor vehicle traffic accidents, policymakers can take a substantial step toward raising U.S. life expectancy to levels comparable to those of most other developed countries. From 1950 to 1970, U.S. life expectancy increased only marginally by less than three years. A modest decrease in life expectancy inequality also occurred. Then, between 1970 and 1980, life expectancy quickly increased, increasing by three years in just a decade. The disparity in life expectancy decreased quickly. Before 1970, the main trend was increased cardiovascular mortality, fueled by various factors such as dietary changes and more sedentary occupations. However, in the 1970s, sharp drops in cardiovascular and cerebrovascular mortality occurred due to more aggressive and successful blood pressure control.

The Causes of Low Lifespan and the High Lifespan in the United States

Some Americans might dispute the nation's racial history, the results of recent presidential elections, the effectiveness of vaccines, war atrocities, internal uprisings, and climate change. Americans cannot ignore that the U.S. has a lower birth expectancy than other developed nations.

United States is the top member of the OECD (Organisation for Economic Co-operation and Development). The top 20 countries in life expectancy still need to make a list. In 2020, countries such as Iceland, Israel, Japan, Norway, Sweden, and Switzerland had life expectancies between 83 and 85 years, compared to 77 years in the United States. Canada, Italy, France, Germany, Greece, Spain, and the United Kingdom are among the countries having much greater life expectancies than America.

In 2020, COVID-19 contributed to a 16 percent rise in the death rate by causing roughly 375,000 deaths in the United States, worsening the country's mortality. COVID-19 ranked third among the leading causes of death, accounting for 11% of the approximately 3.4 million fatalities in 2020. It was followed by unintentional injuries caused by drug overdoses, car accidents, and falls, at a rate of 6%, and preceded by heart disease and cancer, at 21 and 18%, respectively.

The most significant decline in life expectancy since World War II was caused by COVID-19, which reduced America's life expectancy at birth by a few years. It's anticipated that the decrease will last for at least another year.

Income also affects life expectancy, with the poor having shorter lives than the wealthy. The disparity in life expectancy at birth between the poorest and wealthiest Americans is 15 years for males and ten years for women.

America's short life expectancy at birth results from several interrelated social, economic, and political issues. They include a lack of universal health coverage, a public health emergency, inadequate federal drug regulation, and bad lifestyle choices exacerbating chronic illnesses.

The United States continues to be an outlier in that it does not have universal healthcare coverage compared to other advanced developed nations. Many Americans are not receiving the necessary medical care due to the high and steadily rising costs of medical care and health insurance, as well as the lack of insurance for about 50 million Americans.

One challenging unhealthy lifestyle in America is cigarette smoking. With about one in seven American adults being a smoker, smoking is the leading cause of preventable deaths. It is responsible for nearly 500,000 deaths yearly, and smokers die ten years earlier than nonsmokers.

In addition to smoking, other notable unhealthy lifestyles contributing to chronic illnesses and premature deaths are obesity, alcohol misuse, and drug overdoses. America has the highest rate of adult obesity among OECD nations, at around 42 percent in 2018.

Additionally, life expectancy among European nations has fluctuated at various points, sometimes coinciding with significant wars and periods of economic hardship in European history. Contrarily, the health disparity in the US started to become apparent halfway through the century and has only worsened since then, which is remarkable given that this period was marked by unprecedented economic growth and stability. This raises concerns about particular elements of post-war America that might be to blame for the poor health of Americans.

Americans have both higher mortality and morbidity than men and women in other high-income countries. Second, the US health disadvantage begins at birth and extends throughout life. Third, the lag in US life expectancy is particularly large for American women. Finally, the US health disadvantage is most pronounced in the Midwest and Southeast regions of the US.

Both men and women have age-standardized mortality rates from specific causes that are abnormally high in their young and middle years. Compared to almost every other OECD nation, the US has greater mortality rates from infectious diseases, complications during pregnancy, childbirth, and the puerperium, and ailments that develop during the perinatal period. Around 1980, differences in some causes began to emerge; for instance, in recent decades, the difference between accidental poisoning and transport accidents has grown significantly due to larger declines in other countries coupled with rising or stagnant trends in the US. Contrarily, homicide mortality in the US has consistently been higher for several decades, consistent with earlier data showing significantly higher rates of firearm-related deaths in the US.

Chapter Eight

Life Expectancy in the Africa Continent

"The region's commitment to enhancing population health and well-being is evidenced by the sharp increase in healthy life expectancy over the previous two decades. According to Dr. Matshidiso Moeti, WHO Regional Director for Africa, "at its core, Its essence is that more people are living longer, healthier lives with fewer threats from infectious diseases and better access to care and disease prevention services. However, development must continue. The gains in health could be at risk if nations don't step up their efforts to combat the threat of cancer and other non-communicable diseases

If effective catch-up plans are not implemented, the impact of the COVID-19 pandemic may also undermine advancements in healthy life expectancy. Compared to other regions, African nations generally reported more service disruptions. More than 90% of the 36 nations that responded to a WHO survey in 2021 reported one or more disruptions to essential health services, with higher disorders in immunization, neglected tropical diseases, and nutrition services.

There have been efforts to restore vital services compromised by the pandemic. Governments must increase public health funding to improve health services and ensure they are adequate, high-quality, and accessible. Most African governments fund less than fifty percent of their national health budgets, resulting in substantial financing gaps. Only Algeria, Botswana, Cabo Verde, Eswatini, Gabon, Seychelles, and South Africa allocate more than 50 percent of their national healthcare expenditures. Healthcare costs are not deemed catastrophic when families spend less than 10% of their income on health care, regardless of their poverty level. In 15 nations, out-of-pocket expenditures have stagnated or increased during the previous two decades.

According to a World Health Organization (WHO) evaluation, Africa's average healthy life expectancy has improved by ten years per person between 2000 and 2019. This increase is greater than anything seen in any other part of the world over the same period. The report also mentions that the COVID-19 pandemic's disruptive effects may jeopardize these significant advancements.

The global population of adults aged 60 and older is predicted to increase, including in Africa. This results from factors that extend life expectancies, such as decreased population growth, decreased fecundity, and improved medical interventions.

While this is typical for developed countries, it is not the same for Africa and similar developing regions. In these regions, a significant proportion of death is due to non-communicable diseases (NCDs) such as hypertension, cerebrovascular accident, coronary heart disease, diabetes mellitus, chronic renal disease, and cancer. The rising prevalence of NCDs due mainly to western style diets and sedentary living is made worse by inadequate nutrition education, high prevalence of low birth weight, poor health services, lack of efficient tobacco control, and poor planning of the built environment. To halt the possible reduction in life expectancy occasioned by NCDs, efforts by the community, health planners, and African governments to address relevant NCDs must be implemented.

Suggested measures are:

- Nutrition education.

- Regular community-directed physical exercise.

- Improved environmental planning and development.

Others include a review of the current health care system, early NCD identification, prevention, and treatment, improved antenatal care to prevent low birth weights, and the integration of policies and procedures that restrict access to cigarettes, particularly for women of childbearing age. Due to NCDs and their complications, Africa and other developing regions cannot pay the health bill; therefore, this epidemic must be treated seriously.

HIV/AIDS, TB, and maternal mortality are the leading causes of death between the ages of 5 and 60 (in comparison to nations with higher incomes) (i.e., deaths in childbirth).

Since the ICPD Programme of Action was adopted, Sub-Saharan Africa has seen the biggest absolute increase in life expectancy at birth, rising from 49.1 years in 1994 to 61.1 years in 2016.

In 2022, males born in Lesotho will have the lowest life expectancy in the world. Similarly low is the female life expectancy in this country. The average lifespan of a woman is 56 years. Girls born in Nigeria had the lowest life expectancy in the world in 2022, with only 54 years.

Africa has historically had a fairly low life expectancy, but in recent years, the continent's life expectancy has increased.

In African nations, the average life expectancy has increased from 20% to 42% since 2000. That represents the largest increase in life expectancy during that period across all geographical areas. Malawi has experienced one of the largest rises in life expectancy. In 2000, Malawi had a life expectancy of 44.1 years. According to a 2014 report, Malawi's new life expectancy was 62.7 years, a 42.2 percent increase.

One of the primary contributors to the rise in life expectancy in Africa has been improvements in health and welfare. The HIV/AIDS epidemic is one of the worst health problems that Africa has ever faced. In Africa, HIV/AIDS has sadly claimed many lives, one of the main reasons life expectancy is so low. Treating these diseases was difficult at the height of the epidemic, so many

Africans died. Because HIV/AIDS has been such a huge issue, much research has been done to help alleviate the problem. Improvements in medication and treatment have helped Africans and others worldwide combat the AIDS epidemic. Not only is there now medicine available to help suppress the disease, but this medicine has become much more affordable for all people, including those in developing countries.

In Africa, malaria was another problem that reduced life expectancy. But since then, steps have also been taken to address that problem. According to World Health Organization statistics (WHO), malaria cases have dropped 66 percent in Africa since 2000. More significantly, malaria cases among African children under five have dropped by 71%. This is significant because more children in Africa are surviving. Before these advancements, malaria and HIV/AIDS took the lives of youngsters under five. More children have lived past five years in Africa due to improved access to healthcare. It's much more likely that these kids will succeed after completing their first five years of life once they reach 60.

At the dawn of the twentieth century, Sub-Saharan Africa was characterized by extremely high under-five mortality levels and low life expectancy at birth. By the end of the century, however, mortality among children under five had decreased from about 500 per 1,000 live births to about 150 (World Bank 2005). One of the major achievements of the twentieth century in Sub-Saharan Africa is the unprecedented decline in mortality and the corresponding increase in the expectation of life at birth.

In the 1960s, the infant mortality rate in Sub-Saharan Africa was 149 per 1,000 live births to about 101 in 2005—a 32 percent decline over 35 years. Toward the end of the last decade of the twentieth century, the decline in infant mortality rates leveled off, decreasing only slightly for the region.

Regarding subregional differences, West Africa and Middle Africa have continuously had the highest infant mortality rates since 1960. (table 2.3). Middle Africa presently has the highest incidence of infant mortality since West Africa's rate of decline was a little faster. The infant mortality rates in Southern African nations are the lowest of any Sub-Saharan African subregions. For instance, the infant mortality rate in Southern Africa was less than half the average for Sub-Saharan Africa in 2000, even with rising overall mortality in the 1990s. In 1960, the rate was 42% lower than in other subregions.

Reasons For Premature Death In Sub-Saharan Africa.

In contrast to 1990, a higher proportion of healthy years were lost in most of Sub-Saharan Africa in 2010 due to disability. In Sub-Saharan Africa, however, infectious diseases such as HIV/AIDS and malaria accounted for a larger proportion of disability than in the rest of the world. The top causes of impairment in the region, including depression and low back pain, were comparable to the leading causes worldwide. Nearly twice as many people died from nutritional deficiencies in Sub-Saharan Africa in 2010 as they did globally. Lower-income countries primarily drove this trend; upper-middle-income countries in the region, such as Mauritius and Seychelles, were not affected by it.

In Sub-Saharan Africa, malnutrition and household air pollution were among the main risk factors for early death and disability. Childhood underweight, inadequate breastfeeding, and vitamin deficiencies have decreased by between 30 and 50 percent in most countries during the past two decades. Nonetheless, these risk factors remain among the region's top three causes of health loss, particularly in low-income nations.

In many Sub-Saharan African nations, drinking alcohol, having high blood pressure, and smoking were major causes of health decline.

There needs to be more data on cause-specific mortality in Sub-Saharan Africa. Estimates were often derived largely from independent disease-specific epidemiological studies. They were not examined within the context of an overall demographic "envelope" of mortality, as is required to ensure that claims about causes of death are not exaggerated.

In the previous decade, significant advancements have been accomplished in collecting mortality statistics from various sources. These include data from previously existing sources uncovered during a systematic search and data from new data collection ventures established to fill these data gaps.

The World Health Organization (WHO) conducted a comprehensive search for these data over the period 2001–02 as part of the data collection for the GBD 2000 project (Kowal, Rao, and Mathers 2003). Few countries in Africa have vital registration systems that are more than 50 percent complete. Coverage is about this level in Kenya and Zimbabwe (Lopez et al. 2002) and close to 90 percent in South Africa (Dorrington et al. 2001). In Mozambique, a major exercise was undertaken to improve mortality registration and cause-of-death attribution in four cities (Cliff et al. 2003). As expected, the highest proportion of deaths among children under five is from group 1 causes (perinatal conditions, infectious diseases, and malnutrition), ranging from 75 percent in the South African data set to 94 percent in the data from Zambia. A reassuring feature of these vital records data is the relatively low proportion of deaths not classified in any of the three cause groups.

In global comparisons, this shift in cause composition across ages is less evident in Sub-Saharan Africa than in other regions due to the catastrophic HIV/AIDS epidemic. At ages 5 to 14 years, the South African data set suggests a low proportion of deaths due to the causes. This may be because the population covered by registration is urban, with higher socioeconomic status (expressed as GDP per capita) than the national average.

Road Accidents, Epidemics Outbreaks, And Wars As Factors Affecting Human Life Expectancy In Parts Of Sub-Saharan Africa.

Africa has the world's highest road traffic injury (RTI) fatality rate; RTIs are anticipated to become the top cause of death for children five to fifteen years old and the second largest cause of premature mortality among young men after HIV/AIDS. The endemic problem of RTIs, which disproportionately affects the socioeconomically impoverished in Sub-Saharan Africa, is aggravated by limited access to healthcare and limited resources and infrastructure to address this problem effectively. Moreover, losing a family's primary wage earner due to an RTI can devastate the family and represent a significant social and economic catastrophe.

Sub-Saharan Africa's improvements in life expectancy vary across women and men, sub-regions, and countries.

The average lifespan in the African region known as Sub-Saharan is 68 years. The lowest male life expectancy in sub-Saharan Africa is 49 years in the Central African Republic. Cape Verde has seventy-three of the greatest. The respective life expectancy for women in these countries is 55 and 79 years.

In sub-Saharan Africa, the death rate among children under five has decreased dramatically. As a percentage of deaths, the number of children under five has declined from 45% in 1950 to 10% in 2017.

This is likely attributable to multiple initiatives, including the expansion of immunization programs, improvements in water and sanitation, and the widespread distribution of insecticide-treated bed nets. Also contributing to the decline in infant mortality rates are mothers' higher levels of education and rising incomes; however, it is imperative to exercise caution.

It is no longer inevitable that funeral costs will continue to decline. Increasing epidemics of hypertension, hyperglycemia and obesity in many African nations may shift in the other direction over the years.

High blood pressure, high blood sugar, breast, and cervical cancer, and obesity are the leading risk factors for death among women aged 50 to 69. The leading risk factors for men within the same age bracket include hypertension, hyperglycemia, prostate cancer, and alcohol consumption.

Some noncommunicable diseases, such as diabetes, heart attacks, and stroke, are anticipated soon to be the leading causes of death in the region.

In Sub-Saharan Africa, communicable diseases and maternal and infant mortality continue to predominate. Significant advancement has been made in reducing the prevalence of infectious diseases and early childhood conditions, particularly diarrheal diseases and respiratory infections. These diseases continue to account for most health losses in the region, but their relative loads have declined significantly over the previous two decades.

Since 1970, Sub-Saharan Africa has made average progress in reducing mortality and extending life expectancy; nevertheless, between 1990 and 2010, many countries demonstrated an increase in mortality rates for specific age groups and sexes. Mozambique, for example, has shown an increase in mortality rates among women aged 25 to 29.

The region has successfully reduced premature mortality and disability over the past two decades due to several communicable, newborn, nutritional, and maternal causes, particularly diarrheal illnesses and lower respiratory infections. Since 1990, the neighborhood's mortality from measles and tetanus has decreased significantly. Malaria and HIV/AIDS were responsible for a greater decline in fitness in 2010 than in 1990; however, both diseases peaked between 2000 and 2005 in most countries.

Conflicts over basic resources such as food and water, access to and control over rich minerals, unresolved political issues, and agendas, the impact of the worldwide economic crisis, rising costs of living, human rights violations, land and border disputes, harsh dictatorship, high unemployment particularly amongst educated youths all contribute to the escalation of warfare in many developing nations, particularly in Sub-Saharan Africa.

It has been suggested that corrupt practices significantly affect food safety and life expectancy in developing nations. Poverty, starvation, and extreme food insecurity plaguing the masses are not due to a lack of resources but to the absence of a "messiah," a true patriot, or selfless counselors and managers of national resources and taxpayer funds.

Disruption of health care and education, high prevalence of gastrointestinal and respiratory infections (pneumonia, tuberculosis, dysentery, and cardiovascular diseases), malnutrition, maternal vitamin deficiency, increased number of refugees, and youth mortality and morbidity are indirect effects of war. Existing malnutrition in Africa is aggravated by war conditions, increasing mortality and morbidity.

The problem of refugees is one of the unfortunate consequences of war. There were about 9 million refugees and internally displaced individuals in Sub-Saharan Africa due to the conflict. At some point during the Vietnam War, the large number of refugees resulted in a lack of medical equipment and inadequate preservation capacity, requiring 150 Vietnamese physicians to care for 15 million civilians.

Therefore, life expectancy became approximately 35 years, half of the children born died before their fifth birthday, and infant mortality reached 225 per 1000 live births. Pre-war acute malnutrition in Liberia was 1.6%, but during the conflict in December 1989, malnutrition increased between 10 and 50%. Periodically, malnutrition increases proportionately to the scale of the battle and the relocation of portions of the population. Similar patterns were observed in Somalia, Sudan, and numerous other countries.

In Sub-Saharan African nations, good governance, equity, peaceful coexistence, acknowledgment of human rights, and proper food provision will assist in eradicating malnutrition and preventing conflict.

Chapter Nine

Environmental Degradation as a Factor That Affects the Human Lifespan

Aside from gender and genetic information, environmental factors also include outside forces that affect aging.

The environment can significantly influence a person's longevity. Environmental factors that shorten life expectancy include pollutants, poor diet, and stress. This may sound like common sense, but often we only realize these things once it's too late.

Toxins are one example. Everyone would agree that ingesting pesticides is harmful. But what about eating high-fat and high-salt foods? Is eating fast food every day, or even every week, good for you? And we are just talking about fat and salt. This does not include the other chemicals used in their processing and packaging.

Socioeconomic, dietary, lifestyle, genetic, and environmental factors can influence an entire country's health and lifespan. Environmental degradation may also be one of the factors affecting life expectancy. In many nations, environmental degradation poses a threat to rising life expectancy.

The World Health Organization estimates that 4.2 million premature deaths worldwide occurred in 2016 because of ambient air pollution. That number is expected to rise because 90% of people worldwide live in areas with poor air quality. Environmental degradation can adversely impact population health in several ways. Severe outdoor air pollution is responsible for rising chronic diseases (e.g., Asthma, heart diseases, and lung cancer) and increasing premature mortality. Others concluded that environmental degradation increases the likelihood of waterborne diseases such as malaria and dengue fever.

Environmental degradation might lead to negative variations in food production and water quality, contributing to higher mortality, especially among infant and elderly populations and vulnerable people from lower socioeconomic backgrounds. As a result, environmental degradation might increase the variability in the ecosystem, increasing the probability of floods and droughts. Wen, Gu, and Wang et al. discovered that poor air quality significantly impacts older people's longevity because they cannot deal with environmental degradation due to other comorbidities.

Care for the environment shows concern for the future, whether for one's own or future generations. Yet, life expectancy plays a significant role in determining how people value the future: a longer life expectancy makes people more empathetic toward future generations and their future selves. If a person anticipates living longer, she should be willing to invest more in environmental quality.

The causal relationship between life expectancy and environmental quality could also be inverted. Several medical and epidemiological studies, such as Elo and Preston (1992), Pope (2000), Pope et al. (2004), and Evans and Smith (2005), demonstrate that the quality of the environment is a significant factor affecting health and morbidity: air and water pollution, depletion of natural resources, soil deterioration, and the like, are all capable of increasing human mortality (thus reducing longevity).

Therefore, it should not be surprising that life expectancy positively correlates with environmental quality across nations. The data also imply the existence of "convergence clubs" in terms of longevity and environmental performance, with countries clustered around two levels of life expectancy and environmental quality, respectively.

In a drive to achieve higher economic growth, these developing nations exert great pressure on environmental resources, and their expanding production contributes to higher CO2 emissions and industrial wastes. Countries with high levels of environmental degradation cannot achieve the long-term economic and health benefits of strong environmental laws. Their disregard for the environment demands more examination. A study to date has yet to explore the determinants of life expectancy in the most polluted nations while considering the negative impact of environmental degradation on the population's longevity. This encourages us to undertake this research to fill the current research void.

Longevity and sanitation are related. Life expectancy is decreased due to the spread of numerous diseases, such as cholera, dysentery, hepatitis A, typhoid, etc., due to poor sanitation. This data shows that inadequate sanitation is a major cause of almost 432,000 fatalities annually. Similarly, contaminated or filthy drinking water spreads diseases that reduce life expectancy through neonatal mortality.

According to a WHO report, 485 000 people die from diarrhea yearly, most often due to contaminated water. To assess the health status and quality of life in lower-middle and low-income nations, Islam et al. examined data on healthy life expectancy (HALE). They discovered that success in achieving the millennium development goals, economic freedom, the amount of corruption, carbon dioxide emissions, and other known factors are all highly correlated to higher life expectancy.

Malnutrition, insufficient water supply, and environmental pollution pose significant health risks to humans. From an environmental standpoint, a lack of arable land and water stress are significant causes of food insecurity. In light of the current deterioration of human health, contaminated drinking water and indoor air pollution are the most dangerous environmental factors.

Important for providing ecological services, biodiversity is declining at an unprecedented rate. Africa and Asia currently have the highest loss rates. The most significant element of pressure is agricultural expansion. Future climate change could also pose a substantial threat to biodiversity. The potential solutions are the expansion of protected areas, the reduction of land conversion due to increased agriculture, and the cessation of roadside encroachment.

The achievement of the Millennium Development Goal to end hunger and the preservation of biodiversity appear incompatible.

Agriculture puts upward pressure on the demand for arable land. This demand may increase further if the international biofuel market develops. Moving to more intense practices may offset the need to expand agricultural land.

However, higher yields are often associated with higher air, water, and soil emissions. Increasing inputs of nutrients in agriculture results in eutrophication of inland water bodies and coastal waters and poses risks to health and fresh water and marine ecosystems (algae blooms, "dead zones"). Good agricultural practices can limit these impacts.

Over 12 million people worldwide die annually due to bad living and working conditions. 1 Healthful Persons The 2030 Agenda focuses on minimizing people's exposure to dangerous pollutants in the air, water, soil, food, and building materials.

Our environment provides various benefits, including the atmosphere we breathe, the meals we eat, the water we consume, and the numerous items we need in our homes, work, and recreation.

Environmental Pollutants can cause respiratory disorders, heart disease, and certain types of cancer. Low-income individuals are more prone to reside in polluted locations with dangerous drinking water. And children and pregnant women are more susceptible to pollution-related health issues.

Predominantly from X-rays or CT scans, although the radiation for different procedures varies widely, the benefit usually outweighs the risk. Radon occurs naturally in the ground, and areas such as Cornwall have high levels, contributing to higher levels of lung cancer, but these risks are still relatively small. We are also exposed to radiation when flying. A transatlantic return flight is the equivalent of one Chest X-ray. However, this amount of radiation is still extremely small, and unless you traveled extensively, it would have very little overall effect. There has been a lot of debate around the effect of 'wireless radiation' from high mobile phone use. The jury is still out, and the WHO has categorized it as 'possibly carcinogenic, but the Health Protection Agency has found no consistent evidence that it is harmful.

Human health and well-being are inextricably related to environmental conditions. Regarding clean air and water, fertile land for food production, and energy and material inputs for production, high-quality natural ecosystems satisfy fundamental requirements.

Climate And Geographical Problems

In addition to causing death and sickness through increasingly frequent extreme weather events such as heatwaves, storms, and floods, climate change is already causing disruptions in food systems, increases in zoonoses and food-, water-, and vector-borne diseases, and mental health difficulties. In addition, climate change undermines various socioeconomic determinants of health, such as means of subsistence, equality, and access to health care and social support networks. Women, children, members of minority groups, economically deprived areas, refugees and other migrants, the elderly, and people with preexisting health conditions are disproportionately impacted by climate-sensitive health concerns.

Climate change is the greatest health hazard to humans, and health experts worldwide actively respond to the resulting health risks. The global temperature increase must be limited to 1.5°C. Past emissions have already rendered inevitable a certain degree of global temperature rise and other climatic impacts. However, even global warming of 1.5°C is not considered safe; each additional tenth of a degree will have grave consequences for people's lives and health.

Although no one is immune to these risks, the people whose health is impacted the most by the climate crisis are those who have contributed the least to its causes and are least able to defend themselves and their families from it: those in low-income countries and communities.

The effects of climate change on the social and environmental determinants of health — clean air, safe drinking water, sufficient food, and safe shelter – are significant.

Malnutrition, malaria, diarrhea, and heat stress are anticipated to cause roughly 250 000 more fatalities annually between 2030 and 2050 due to climate change.

In conjunction with other natural and anthropogenic health stressors, climate change significantly affects human health and disease. Some known health threats will intensify, while new ones may arise. Not all individuals are equally in danger. Age, economic resources, and geography are important factors to consider.

Physical, biological, and ecological disruptions, including domestic and international disturbances, can impact public health in the United States. The health effects of these disruptions include an increase in respiratory and cardiovascular disease, injuries and premature deaths associated with extreme weather events, changes in the prevalence and geographic distribution of food- and waterborne infections and other infectious illnesses, and threats to mental health.

Researchers have long observed that residents of particular regions of the United States live many years longer than those in other regions. A group of researchers designed a comprehensive study to understand better why this occurs, whether it is rising or decreasing, and which factors may contribute to variances in longevity.

According to NPR, the disparity in life expectancy between counties in the United States mirrors the discrepancies between lifespans in the world's low- and high-income regions. The 20-year discrepancy in life expectancy found by this U.S. study appears to be influenced by socioeconomic standing. Residents of regions with a high life expectancy, such as Summit County, Colorado, are among the nation's wealthiest and most educated. In contrast, residents of regions with a short life expectancy, such as Oglala Lakota County, South Dakota, or portions of southern Mississippi and eastern Kentucky, are significantly poorer and have a lower level of education.

Many view it as a call to action while highlighting various problems. Professionals in public health can undertake specific activities and policies to assist in bridging the gap.

According to NPR, smoking and obesity have contributed considerably to the decline in life expectancy in some of the hardest-hit regions. In their lifetimes, all humans experience climate variability and change, regardless of their geographic locations. Seasonal cycles are the most recognizable and predictable phenomena to which people adapt their attire, outdoor activities, thermostat settings, and agricultural techniques. In the same location, however, no two summers or winters are identical; some are warmer, wetter, or stormier than others. Interannual climate variance contributes to year-to-year fluctuations in fuel prices, crop yields, road maintenance budgets, and wildfire dangers. Single-year, precipitation-driven floods can cause catastrophic economic devastation and loss of life, as was the case in the upper Mississippi River drainage basin in the summer of 1993 and throughout much of Bangladesh during the summer of 1998. Wildfires, severe storms, hurricanes, heat waves, and other climate-related catastrophes can also result in comparable property loss and loss of life.

Solar radiation drives the Earth's climate system; seasonal variances in climate are ultimately a result of seasonal changes in Earth's orbit. Air circulation in the atmosphere and ocean water react to seasonal changes in the Sun's available energy.

Chapter Ten

Food/Diet/Nutrition as a Factor That Affects Human Lifespan

Everyone desires a longer lifespan. And we are often advised that the key to achieving this is choosing healthy lifestyle choices, such as engaging in physical activity, avoiding tobacco, and limiting alcohol consumption. Additionally, studies have shown that food can extend longevity.

A new study indicated that eating healthy might add six to seven years to the lifetime of middle-aged adults and ten years to the longevity of young ones. Only some mechanisms that explain why nutrition can increase lifespan are completely understood. However, the ideal diet that the author identified in this book comprises a variety of antioxidant-rich foods. Several studies on human cells indicate that these chemicals may reduce or prevent cell damage, one of the causes of aging. However, this study area is still in its infancy, so it is still being determined whether antioxidants consumed as part of a healthy diet would have the same effect. Many foods in this book contain anti-inflammatory effects, which may help delay the onset of numerous diseases and the aging process.

Changing your diet drastically might be challenging. However, adopting some of the items proven to promote longevity may still be beneficial.

Women and men in the United States, China, and Europe might boost their life expectancy by better than a decade by adopting a healthy diet at age 20. They also discovered that switching from a Western diet to an optimum one at age 60 would add eight years to one's life expectancy. The life expectancy of 80-year-olds might grow by about three and a half years. Accelerated aging is connected with malnutrition. Maintaining a balanced diet is among the numerous essential factors influencing healthy aging.

Healthy eating habits and proper nutrition involve not only the intake of food but also its absorption, digestion, biosynthesis, catabolism, and excretion. Due to poor oral health, inability to chew, tongue dryness, and decreased appetite, the elderly tend to have more difficulty digesting and absorbing food, consume less nutrient-rich foods, and are at a greater risk for malnutrition.

Insufficient nutrient consumption can result in deficiency-related disorders, such as anemia, weakness, and blindness. Age-related chronic diseases include osteoporosis, cardiovascular disease, and diabetes. A decline in healthy eating habits for nutrient-dense foods (i.e., vegetables and fruits) and increased carbohydrate consumption have been shown in older adults with poor dental health or tooth loss. High carbohydrate consumption can increase the risk of diabetes and other comorbidities.

According to Audre Biciunaite, the effect of food availability on mortality is the most evident reason for the correlation between life expectancy and income. There have historically been statistically significant correlations between food prices and mortality."

Beginning at a young age with a good diet leads to the largest increases in life expectancy. Inadequate nutrition can compromise our everyday health and well-being and our ability to live fulfilling and active lives.

Poor nutrition can contribute to stress, fatigue, our ability to function in the short term, and the chance of developing certain diseases and other health problems in the long run.

Poor dietary habits are considered the second-leading risk factor for mortality and disability-adjusted life-years (DALYs) worldwide. Dietary patterns differ based on cultural, environmental, technological, and economic factors. Nutritional deficiencies of energy, protein, and specific micronutrients have contributed to depressed immune function and increased susceptibility to infections.

Dietary patterns differ based on cultural, environmental, technological, and economic factors. However, Dietary patterns are becoming similar due to increasing living standards and the growing globalization of the food sector.

Food causes 45% of all heart diseases — the number one killer in the United States. Food causes 30–35% of all cancers — the number two killer and one skyrocketing in lockstep with our waistlines and likely to overtake heart disease in the coming year.

Since the beginning of time, humans have endeavored to improve the quality of life and extend their longevity. The processes that regulate aging and life expectancy are influenced by genetic, environmental, behavioral, and dietary variables, making longevity a very complicated phenomenon. Although a long-lasting elixir has not yet been discovered, physicians and scientists agree that nutrition significantly impacts general mortality and morbidity and is, therefore, the topic of extensive scientific study.

The dream of eternal youth dates back to humanity's earliest beginnings and is associated with the holy, myth, alchemy, and magic. Even in our modern technological era, this desire has remained the same, and thanks to scientific study, we are attempting to achieve, if not immortality, at least a healthy lifespan. "Let meals be thy medication, and medication be thy food," declared Hippocrates (460 BC - 377 BC), the father of medicine, as the first person to recognize the significance of appropriate nutrition in preserving health. A growing body of evidence, especially in the last several decades, confirms that promoting a balanced diet and a healthy lifestyle is the most effective formula for successful aging.

All living species undergo a multifactorial, gradual, universal, and irreversible aging process. This phenomenon is characterized by multiple changes in organ function, energy metabolism, and cell physiology. It is associated with a diminished capacity to respond to environmental stress, thereby increasing the likelihood of developing chronic diseases, the ultimate causes of death and disability.

The consumption of fewer proteins and amino acids is emerging as a possible intervention for promoting healthy longevity. For example, a recent analysis of the National Health and Nutrition Examination Survey (NHANES) revealed that a drop in protein intake was associated with a reduction in the overall mortality rate among adults younger than 65. In addition, those who consumed over 20% of their calories from proteins had a 4-fold greater risk of cancer mortality and a 75% increase in overall mortality compared to those who consumed less than 10%. In contrast, a plant-based derived protein source diet eliminated the relationship between high protein intake and mortality while attenuating its effect on cancer mortality.

If you deal directly with older seniors, you've likely been asked about meals that promote longevity and keep aging individuals looking and feeling young. Fortunately, many studies demonstrate that nutrition can significantly impact longevity, and many individuals report positive outcomes from minor dietary modifications. It is always possible to make improvements. Adults over 50 can make adjustments today that will enhance their health tomorrow and may help them live longer and in better health.

People tend to consume less food and have less diverse eating behaviors as they age. This is caused to numerous circumstances, such as loss of appetite, altered taste, tooth/denture difficulties, pharmaceutical side effects, eating on a budget, and reliance on institutional meals. Consequently, it is crucial to optimize nutrient-dense diets in later years.

Across the globe, there has been a marked increase in longevity, but significant inequalities remain. These are exacerbated by inadequate access to nutrition and health care services and reliable information to make nutrition and health care decisions. Many economically developing and developed societies are plagued with the double burden of energy excess and undernutrition. This has led to mental and physical decline, increasing prevalence of non-communicable diseases, decreased productivity, increased medical costs, and reduced quality of life. While adequate nutrition is fundamental to good health at all life course stages, the impact of diet on prolonging good quality of life during aging remains to be determined. For progress to continue, there is a need for new and innovative approaches to promoting health as individuals age, as well as qualitative and quantitative biomarkers and other accepted tools that can measure improvements in physiological integrity throughout the life.

People, Lifestyles, And Cultures As Factors Affecting Human Life Expectancy

As the world's population ages, older people are becoming an increasingly important group that merits special attention to health and social issues.

Lifestyles affect health and survival at all ages, but the consequences of poor lifestyle behaviors may differ for older people from younger adults. They can also be heavily dependent on exposure earlier in life. Our current state of knowledge is based predominantly on studies conducted among middle-aged adults or young, older people. Moreover, studies are sparse throughout the entire older age spectrum, from 65 to 90 years.

Behavioral influences play a role, as do psychological influences, which include factors such as personality, attitudes, and beliefs. Many dietary and lifestyle factors are important in the etiology of non-communicable diseases. Such factors include - but are not limited to - food, nutrients, energy intake, physical activity, obesity, smoking, alcohol consumption, behavioral factors (e.g., sleep, stress), and cultural factors.

Cultural concepts of aging are closely related to cultural concepts of time—and many different concepts of time have been described. In more traditional agricultural societies, for example, time is often experienced as more cyclical, or rather spiral, as it is both repetitive and slowly advancing. The religions of these regions, especially in parts of Asia (Nakamura, 1966), often incorporate this cyclical view of human experience and may include concepts of reincarnation such as samsara—the endless cycle of birth, death, and rebirth found in both Buddhism and Hinduism.

Cultural concepts of aging are closely related to cultural concepts of time—and many different concepts of time have been described.

By contrast, the Western world's concept of time as linear has been the basis of intellectual and religious thought for centuries. Joseph Needham (1966) saw this as originating in the Judaeo–Christian worldview, with its sense of time beginning at the creation ex nihilo and ending at the Second Coming or the coming of the Messiah. Western time was conceived as being directional, advancing, and non-repetitive. All human life was a "continuous linear redemptive process," and the history of the world was seen as "a divine drama enacted on a single stage, with no repeat performances." This linear insight of span is apparent in the eighteenth-century philosophes' idea of human progress, the nineteenth-century concepts of social evolution, and the contemporary ideas of developed and developing nations.

Age reflects the effect of biological processes, whereas culture represents the effect of enduring experiences; thus, the combination between age and culture can have various effects on cognition. However, their interplay has yet to be studied. In light of the notion that Asians are more intuitive in their reasoning than Americans, we investigated the interaction between this cultural difference and age. Participants of all ages from the United States and Singapore did a categorization task (living vs. non-living). Suppose performance on a culturally sensitive activity relies mostly on cultural knowledge (rather than cognitive resources). In that case, cultural effects on cognition may be well-maintained during late adulthood, as acquired knowledge (e.g., vocabulary) is less likely to experience standard age-related reductions. Two distinct lines of study initially support this anticipated type of age-culture interaction.

Culture and society can also influence our thoughts and experiences around aging:

In many Western societies, the contemporary notion of 'aging well' presumes independence and active contributions. In many other societies, older adults have been encouraged to disengage and to be looked after. This might appear negative at first thought, but it also means that the notion of dependency is seen as more normal rather than as a source of stigma.

It is important to note that contemporary notions of 'successful aging' can potentially exclude large segments of the older population: those with few materials, health-related and socio-cultural resources, and those who die before they reach 'old age.

Gender, level of education, income, key personality traits, and ethnicity have all been shown to shape the experience of aging among older adults, which can start with something as basic as longevity.

Conclusion

As we read through the book's chapters, we understood what life expectancy is, what it entails, how it is inherited, and how we can link it to a gene. The factors that affect life expectancy around the world were also covered.

Regardless of the shape of the survival curve, the area under the curve can be used to calculate life expectancy. The area between the different survival curves is a gain in life expectancy linked with one health strategy vs. another (or being in one exposure group versus another). To properly evaluate a given gain, it is crucial to determine the baseline risk in the control group and the proportion of individuals expected to benefit from the intervention. It is undoubtedly a fallacy to regard increases in life expectancy as additions of time to the end of a finite lifespan. There are numerous empirical approaches for estimating life expectancy, each with its strengths and weaknesses.

It is hardly unexpected that different high-income nations have varying degrees of life expectancy. The fact that there weren't many high-income countries with significant disparities around 1950, that the divergence detailed in this research started very abruptly around 1980, and that it took so long to identify and evaluate this divergence are even more surprising. When life expectancy trends are compared across nations at different ages, it is evident that there has been a divergence for both men and women at ages above and below 50. Nevertheless, the largest variation among countries appears to have been for women aged 50 and over, and this population segment has been the primary focus of this report.

As people live longer, death ages become more comparable. This dual advancement during the past two centuries, a fundamental objective of public health programs, is a significant achievement of contemporary civilization. Recent exceptions to the concurrent increase in life expectancy and life span equality make it difficult to pinpoint the fundamental causes of this correlation. Using principles regarding the rate and form of aging, we establish a coherent framework for studying the evolution of life expectancy and life span equality.

We examine the dynamic relationship between life expectancy and life span equality using data from the Human Mortality Database for 49 nations and regions, focusing on long-term data from Sweden. This book demonstrates that life expectancy and life span equality changes are weighted sums of mortality reduction progress rates. This result holds for three distinct metrics of lifespan variability. The weights change over time and represent the ages at which mortality decreases boost life expectancy and life span equality: the more progress at the youngest ages, the stronger the association.

As the obesity epidemic has spread, the number of people at risk of obesity-related health problems has risen. At the same time, however, managing some more serious obesity-related health problems, such as heart disorders and type 2 diabetes, has improved. Thus, the net effect of rising obesity on mortality is difficult to estimate.

Although common variability accounts for just 25% of human lifespan variability, knowing the genetic foundation of longevity may provide important recommendations for modifying lifestyle to achieve longevity and increase health span. In other words, a suitable combination of polymorphisms enables a few individuals to have an efficient metabolism or an effective response to various stresses, allowing them to live longer. Others can get a comparable outcome by targeting the same pathways with proper lifestyle choices or therapies. In this setting, the significance of epigenetic variables as indicators of aging and intervention targets will undoubtedly increase shortly.

Our natural environment makes human life possible, and our cultural environment helps define who we are. It is, therefore, essential that our population and economic growth are environmentally sustainable. The most optimistic outlook for our environment is one in which we get the balance between continuing to support and implement effective policies, programs, and resources.

The environment can also play a vital part in determining someone's longevity. Stepping away from gender and genetic information, environmental factors include external influences on aging. Environmental factors, such as toxins, lack of nutrition, and stress, decrease life expectancy. This seems like a no-brainer, except we only sometimes identify these things until it's too late.

We must realize that more can be done, without requiring scientific discovery, to extend longevity and enhance health in the World. Social and environmental factors affect health just as much as physical factors do. Up to half of the premature mortality and morbidity may be attributed to risky health behaviors, a lack of access to healthcare, and unfavorable life circumstances (Rhodes, 2015). The length of healthy life in the US can significantly increase through behavioral changes, social and economic improvements, and policy changes. Our life expectancy in the United States is dramatically below its scientific potential (Crimmins, Preston, & Cohen, 2011). The United States not only ranks very poorly in life expectancy among all countries with incomes like ours, but since 1950 our rank is falling relative to other countries. For women, we have had decades of stagnation in life expectancy, leaving us at the bottom of the group of wealthy and long-lived countries.

Other factors, particularly the rising level of obesity in the United States, also appear to have played a significant part.

However, as noted, there is a good deal of uncertainty in the literature regarding the mortality consequences of obesity and possible trends therein. Several peer-reviewed articles appearing recently suggest effects of quite different orders of magnitude. Preston and Stokes (2010) conclude that even using relatively low estimates of associated risk, obesity accounts for a fifth to a third of the shortfall in life expectancy in the United States relative to other high-income countries.

These changes have usually followed the worldwide patterns the Intergovernmental Panel on Climate Change predicted and outlined in their assessment reports up until now. Extreme occurrences are exceptional due to their magnitude, suddenness, and spectacular character. However, it is impossible to attribute them directly and completely to climate change because, by definition, they are unusual. On a global scale, the scope of climate change includes some extreme occurrences for which an increase in frequency, intensity, and duration is anticipated to have an increasingly significant and perceptible effect on the public, the natural and built environment, and socioeconomic activity. Given the predicted magnitude of climate change, natural and human system responses (adaptation) can adjust and even convert unfavorable and sometimes positive outcomes.

In conclusion, the perceptions and behaviors, the processes and factors leading to decision-making, and the goals and convictions of individuals and communities, appear crucial to the adaptation of human systems, as humans will ultimately make the correct or incorrect decisions affecting the future.

Acknowledging these limitations, the panel's strategy was to try to establish the strength of the evidence for a number of the most commonly proffered explanations for differences in life expectancy between the United States and other high-income countries—for example, that these differences are the result of a particularly inefficient U.S. health care system or that they are a function of poor health behaviors in the United States, particularly concerning smoking, overeating, and failing to exercise sufficiently. The panel also considered differences among countries in levels of social integration and socioeconomic inequality.

This book demonstrates that increased life expectancy in our sample countries is threatened by environmental degradation. According to the findings of this book, we suggest that policymakers in these countries adopt measures to reduce carbon emissions, which will enhance public health and productivity; that environmental-friendly technologies and resources, such as renewable energy, be used in the production process; that healthcare spending on a national budget be increased; and that people in these countries have access to clean drinking water and basic sanitation facilities.

References

https://www.cbsnews.com/amp/philadelphia/news/us-life-expectancy-lowest-in-decades-after-dropping-nearly-a-full-year-in-2021/

Aizer, Anna, and Janet Currie. "The intergenerational transmission of inequality: Maternal disadvantage and health at birth." Science 344, No. 6186 (2014): 856-861.

Almond, Douglas, Janet Currie, and Valentina Duque. "Childhood Circumstances and Adult Outcomes: Act II." July 2017.

Cullen, M., M. Baiocchi, K. Eggleston, et al. "The weaker sex? Vulnerable men and women's resilience to socio-economic disadvantage." SSM- Population Health (2016); 2: 512-524.

Cullen, Mark R., Clint Cummins, and Victor R. Fuchs. "Geographic and racial variation in premature mortality in the U.S.: analyzing the disparities." PLoS One 7.4 (2012): e32930.

Currie, Janet, and Hannes Schwandt. "Mortality inequality: The good news from a county-level approach."Journal of Economic Perspectives 30.2 (2016): 29-52.

Report of the Second World Assembly on Ageing (United Nations Publication A/CONF.197/9, Sales No.02.IV.4).

Bongaarts, J. (2004) Long Range Trends in Adult Mortality Trends: Models and Projection Methods. Population Council Working Paper, 192.

Cutler, D. and Meara, E. (2003) Changes in the Age Distribution of Mortality over the 20th Century. In: Wise, D., Ed., Perspectives on the Economics of Aging, University of Chicago Press, Chicago.

The Borgen project

The world bank in Africa.

ABS (Australian Bureau of Statistics). 2003.

Australia. Vol. 3302. Annual report. Canberra: ABS.

Adetunji, J. A., C. J. Murray, and T. Evans. 1996. "Causes of Death in Africa: A Review." Paper presented at a meeting of the Population Association of America, New Orleans, May.

Black R. E., Morris S. S., Bryce J. *Where and Why Are 10 Million Children Dying Every Year?* Lancet. 2003;361:2226–34. [PubMed]

Brass, W. 1968. *Demography of Tropical Africa.* Princeton, NJ: Princeton University Press.

Cliff, J., J. Sacarlal, O. Augusto, A. Nóvoa, M. Dgedge, G. Machatine, and H. Cossa. 2003. *Estudos das principais causas de morte registadas, nas citades des Maputo, Beira, Chimoio e Nampula, em 2001.* Maputo City, Mozambique: Ministerio de Saude.

A.J. McMichael et al.

Mortality trends and setbacks: global convergence or divergence? Lancet (2004)O. Galor

From stagnation to growth: unified growth theory

M.F. Evans et al.

Do new health conditions support mortality-air pollution effects?

Journal of Environmental Economics and Management.

www.ingramcontent.com/pod-product-compliance
Lightning Source LLC
Chambersburg PA
CBHW051758250726
48659CB00001B/480